Côte à côte 3:
Practice in daily colloquial French

Le français familier au quotidien

Copyright © 2019 par Virginia Institute Press, une SRL Villa Magna

Tous droits réservés. Aucune partie de ce livre ne peut être reproduite ou utilisée sous quelque forme et par quelque moyen que ce soit, électronique ou mécanique, y compris par la photocopie, l'enregistrement, ou par tout système de stockage d'information et de recherche documentaire, sans l'accord écrit de l'éditeur.

Virginia Institute Press révise tous les ouvrages qu'elle publie afin d'assurer une qualité linguistique. Virginia Institute Press n'est pas responsable des erreurs de contenu dans la présente publication. Toute erreur de contenu éventuellement trouvée dans cette publication relève de la seule responsabilité de son auteur ou de ses auteurs, qui approuvent la version finale de leurs propres travaux. Virginia Institute Press et les auteurs ne sont, en aucune manière, responsables de l'utilisation par le lecteur du contenu de cette publication.

Pour plus d'informations, veuillez contacter :
Virginia Institute Press/Villa Magna, LLC
PO Box 68425
Virginia Beach, VA 23471

ISBN : 978-1-940178-46-2
Première édition
Conception de la couverture par Diren Yardimli

Imprimé aux États-Unis d'Amérique

Copyright © 2019 by Virginia Institute Press, a Villa Magna, LLC company

All rights reserved. No part of this book may be reproduced or utilized in any form or by any means, electronic or mechanical, including photocopying, recording, or by any information storage and retrieval system, without permission in writing from the publisher.

Virginia Institute Press edits all works it publishes for linguistic quality. Virginia Institute Press is not responsible for any content errors found in this publication. Any content errors eventually found in this publication are the sole responsibility of its author or authors, who approve the final version of their own work. Neither Virginia Institute Press nor the author or authors are responsible in any way whatsoever for the reader's use of the contents in this publication.

For information, contact:
Virginia Institute Press/Villa Magna, LLC
PO Box 68425
Virginia Beach, VA 23471

ISBN: 978-1-940178-46-2
First edition
Cover design by Diren Yardimli

Printed in the United States of America

Cette page a été laissée intentionnellement blanche
This page intentionally left blank

Table of Contents

Introduction en français 9
Introduction in English 13
Organization of the materials 17
PART ONE 19
ENGLISH IDIOMS 21
I. Selection of similes in English and French 23
II. English idioms using names of animals 27
    1. Birds 27
    2. Dogs 29
    3. Cats 30
    4. Fish 32
    5. Horses 33
    6. Cows and bulls 34
    7. Pigs 35
    8. Monkeys 36
    9. Rats 38
    10. Wild animals 38
    11. Insects 40
    12. Other animals 41
III. English idioms using body parts 43
    1. Arm: 43
    2. Back: 44
    3. Belly: 44
    4. Bones: 45
    6. Chin: 47
    7. Ears: 47
    8. Eyes: 48
    9. Fingers: 49
    10. Feet: 50
    11. Hair: 52
    12. Hands: 52
    13. Head: 53
    14. Heart: 55
    15. Legs: 56
    17. Neck: 59
    18. Nerves: 60
    19. Nose: 61

- 20. Shoulders: 62
- 21. Skin: 63
- 22. Stomach: 64
- 23. Teeth: 65
- 24. Throat: 66
- 25. Thumbs: 66
- 26. Toes: 68
- 27. Tongue: 68

IV. English idioms relating to areas of life and the environment 71
- 1. Business 71
- 2. Clothing 73
- 3. Colors 74
- 4. Drinking and beverages 76
- 5. Food 78
- 6. Furniture and household 82
- 7. Gambling 85
- 8. Health 86
- 9. Money 88
- 10. Music 90
- 11. Nature 93
- 12. Numbers 95
- 13. Religion 97
- 14. Sports 100
- 15. Time 103
- 16. Travel 106

V. Miscellaneous English idioms: 111
- Section 1: 111
- Section 2: 113
- Section 3: 116

RECAPITULATION OF PART ONE 119
MATCHING EXERCISES 119
- A few French similes: 119
- I. SECTION ON ANIMALS 120
- II. SECTION ON BODY PARTS 122
- III. SECTION ON BUSINESS, MONEY, AND GAMBLING   127
- IV. SECTION ON CLOTHING AND COLORS 129
- V. SECTION ON DRINKING AND FOOD 130
- VI. SECTION ON FURNITURE AND HOUSEHOLD 132
- VII. SECTION ON HEALTH AND SPORTS 133

VIII. SECTION ON NATURE, TIME, AND RELIGION	135
IX. SECTION ON MUSIC AND TRAVEL	138
X. SECTION ON MISCELLANEOUS IDIOMS	140
PART TWO	145
FRENCH IDIOMS	147
Section 1:	149
Section 2:	150
Section 3:	152
Annex: Solutions des exercices	169
A Brief Bibliography:	197
Other Books by Virginia Institute Press	199

Jacques Bourgeacq

Introduction en français

Ce livre est le troisième de la série <u>Côte à côte</u>, dont l'objectif principal est de développer chez l'étudiant anglophone le *sentiment* de la langue française en l'aidant à pénétrer la vision ou la logique qui sous-tend les structures particulières à chaque langue, le français et l'anglais. Les différences, parfois étranges lorsqu'elles ne sont considérées que d'un seul point de vue, deviennent acceptables à l'esprit lorsqu'on en comprend la raison. C'est pourquoi l'auteur a choisi pour chaque ouvrage cette approche non seulement comparative, mais aussi cognitive.

<u>Côte à côte 3: Le français familier au quotidien</u> ne fait pas exception. Centré principalement sur la langue parlée, le présent ouvrage a pour but d'offrir à l'étudiant déjà compétent en français de base les moyens d'explorer la langue familière en usage dans la conversation quotidienne chez les Français et les francophones. Que ce soit en anglais ou en français, la communication verbale, essentiellement plus instantanée et plus émotive que l'écrit, réclame souvent l'usage d'images (comparaisons, métaphores) qui confèrent au langage un caractère concret et affectif, visant à mieux capter l'attention sensorielle de l'interlocuteur.

Au cours des siècles, chaque culture a inventé des expressions imagées, appelées *idiotismes* ou *expressions/locutions idiomatiques,* afin de remplacer telle expression abstraite ou *sans éclat* par une autre formulation plus concrète et plus frappante pour l'imagination. Par exemple, au lieu de dire qu'un produit coûte très cher, on pourra dire qu'il « coûte les yeux de la tête »; "a*n arm and a leg,*" dira l'anglophone dans la même situation.

Or il est très rare qu'une expression idiomatique dans une langue corresponde exactement dans une autre langue. Si parfois tel est le cas, c'est le plus souvent que l'un des deux idiotismes a été emprunté à l'autre langue. C'est pourquoi, il est important d'explorer les équivalences entre les deux langues, afin d'en examiner la logique qui les sépare et d'en préserver l'authenticité en communiquant dans la langue étrangère. En fait, le premier volume de <u>Côte à côte</u> avait déjà exploré ce domaine des *équivalences*, dans le chapitre réservé aux « procédés de traduction ». Le présent ouvrage approfondit cette importante question.

On trouvera dans le présent ouvrage un grand nombre d'expressions idiomatiques et leurs équivalences dans l'autre langue. Notre recherche nous a amenés à explorer également leurs origines, afin de mieux les comprendre. Ainsi un vaste corpus d'explications de ces origines, dans chaque langue, servira d'exploration culturelle. Chaque explication apportera également un point de référence utile pour mieux garder l'idiotisme en mémoire.

On notera également que ces idiotismes se sont graduellement « fossilisés » avec l'usage. De ce fait, il n'est donc pas possible de les traduire littéralement d'une langue à l'autre, car dans nombre de cas, ils resteraient incompréhensibles pour quelqu'un qui ne connaîtrait pas les deux langues! Si par exemple je disais en français en buvant ma bière bien fraîche: « Ça frappe la tâche » pour exprimer l'idée de *"It hits the spot,"* mon idiotisme resterait bizarrement impénétrable!

Vu qu'une langue est un réservoir organique de culture, il faut tenir compte du fait que les expressions idiomatiques naissent, vivent un certain temps, puis finissent par disparaître. Certaines durent plus longtemps que d'autres et survivent même parfois pendant des siècles. Nous avons choisi les expressions qui nous paraissaient encore vivantes aujourd'hui. Chaque personne possédant ses idiotismes favoris jugera parfois que tel ou tel idiotisme est périmé, alors qu'une autre l'emploiera encore aujourd'hui. Ce domaine reste donc fluide. En fin de compte, comme nombre d'expressions idiomatiques émaillent parfois les dialogues des œuvres littéraires anciennes, il n'est pas inutile de les comprendre.

Le but visé n'est pas seulement d'apprendre et de pouvoir comprendre et utiliser un certain nombre d'expressions idiomatiques françaises, mais aussi de ***sonder par un processus d'osmose*** la nature et l'ampleur de la vision imaginative française. L'approche cognitive était déjà à la base des deux premiers ouvrages de la série <u>Côte à côte</u>, car pour bien parler une langue, il ne suffit pas de la mémoriser, il faut la sentir.

L'auteur vous souhaite bonne route dans votre exploration de cet aspect pittoresque de la pensée française.

Introduction in English

The first two books of the Côte à côte series explored aspects of *standard* French and English. Continuing our comparative approach, this new volume, Côte à côte 3, is exploring another level of language, more *expressive and imaginative*, which is used more often in spoken exchanges. This level of discourse is characterized by what is customarily called **idioms** (*idiotismes* or *expressions idiomatiques* in French). It frequently uses images, comparisons or metaphors as a means to give abstract ideas a more tangible substance, a more emotional charge. Students should acquire this means of enlivening their own French expression with a moderate and appropriate use of authentic idioms, which most often differ from the conceptions and formulations of their native language. Côte à côte 3 thus pursues the same objective as stated in the first Côte à côte subtitle: it continues to promote « le français tel qu'on le pense », as well as « tel qu'on le parle ».

In the course of History, societies have produced in their respective languages a vast number of special phrases and sentences. Outside of their standard formulations, these phrases and sentences express in colorful terms some glimpses of their collective experience and wisdom. And they apply them to new situations at hand.([1]) Such phrases and sentences are so familiar and so "*natural*" to each of us in our own native language, that we use them instinctively in our daily verbal interactions with peers, and understand them when uttered by others. So much so that we are often even unaware of the special status of these expressions, and especially of their origins. Aside from their expressivity, we also draw some authority from tapping the collective wisdom and discernment of our culture, past and present.

---

1   Collective, popular experience, anonymous in contrast with individually authored statements, such as maxims.

Among such expressions, we find **proverbs** or **adages** (*A bird in the hand is worth two in the bush*); and **sayings**, usually shorter (*to be in the dog house*). These colorful expressions are recognizable as *idioms* insofar as they are not meant to be understood literally, but metaphorically: nobody believes it actually *rains cats and dogs*.

These expressions often present themselves in a "*frozen*" or "*fossilized*" form. For instance, if we heard someone say that an expensive item "*cost the eyes of the head,*" we may of course understand that what was meant is rather "*It cost an arm and a leg.*" The unpleasant feeling of a high cost is identical in both cultures, with both putting a high price tag on some parts of the body, but not necessarily the same. The first expression reflects a literal rendition of what a fluent French speaker would say in this situation: « *Cela coûte les yeux de la tête* ». ("*It costs the eyes of the head*").

We must expect that among the hundreds upon hundreds of idiomatic expressions that we know in our own language very few will coincide exactly in another language. This is due to the fact that each culture has its own particular collective vision and linguistic tradition. An equivalent image in another language will most often come from a different realm of reality. For example, reacting to an unbelievable statement, one may use the idiom "*It does not hold water,*" which is expressed in French as « *Ça ne tient pas debout* » ("*It does not stand erect*").

By contrast, whenever one particular expression coincides in two languages, chances are one was borrowed from the other, or derived from a common source. For example, the French phrase « *lune de miel* » traces back to the English composite word "*honeymoon,*" adapted of course to respect the French syntax. An example of the reverse case is the expression "*a flea market,*" which was borrowed from the French « *marché aux puces* ». In both examples, the images have been preserved, and the syntax has changed according to the grammatical norms of each language. The expressions have been "*naturalized*" so to speak.

It must be expected though that the numerous equivalences between English and French presented in this book will often show images that are far apart, and often puzzling or disconcerting, thus requiring some form of explanation. This is why we have included a vast corpus of brief explanations about the source and history of certain idioms, many of which came to us from the distant past. We also felt that knowing the *how* and the *why* of such expressions can be intellectually stimulating and, as a result, helpful toward their retention.

Some translated equivalents, as found in the dictionaries or on the internet, may have a different connotation than the corresponding idioms. For example, the French proverb « *Il ne faut pas mélanger les torchons et les serviettes* » (meaning literally "*Let's separate dish cloths from napkins*") is indicated in several websites as: "*Don't mix apples and oranges.*" However, this English idiom can apply to a large number of issues and situations, while the French expression is more restricted, referring almost always to social status. It describes rather a difference in social, professional background or attitude between persons or social classes. As such, it might be better translated as "*You have to separate the sheep from the goats*" (a Biblical saying).

Due to the passage of time or the lack of written records, the origins of some idioms are mere speculation, or sometimes the object of several competing theories. So, throughout the book, we have endeavored to point out to such cases, or opted for what appeared to be the most probable or plausible theory.

It may also happen at times that an idiom in one language has no precise equivalent idiom in the other. For instance, "*to beat a dead horse*" (meaning to state the obvious or stressing the obsolete) has no apparent idiomatic equivalent in French and may thus be translated with a periphrase: « *s'acharner inutilement* » ("*to strive in vain*"). The etymology of acharner is la chair (flesh): the original connotation of voracity attached etymologically to the verb s'acharner, evoking carnivorous predators, has practically disappeared, leaving mostly the abstract idea of obstinacy. Therefore, it is no longer felt as an idiom.

One source proposes a French equivalent idiom for "*to beat a dead horse:*" « *Enfoncer une porte ouverte* » (*to force an open door down*). The problem, however, is that the English expression means to waste time and energy on an <u>obsolete</u> issue, while the French idiom means instead to waste energy on a <u>current</u> problem that has already been solved and no longer exists.

There are also expressions like « *lancer un coup d'épée dans l'eau* » ("*to thrust a sword in water*"), but who uses a sword today? All the above expressions show <u>the importance of the context</u> in the choice of an equivalent in another language. At times, it poses a real challenge to the imagination and thus requires a sense of the appropriate and a bit of creativity.

Our choice of idioms was subjectively based on the author's dual (English/French) knowledge of idiom equivalents, as well as their apparent frequent use. It is hoped that readers will be stimulated enough to research the websites and bilingual anthologies for their own favorite idioms not listed in our collection. Thus our book is presented as an invitation to pursue further research.

As language is an organic reservoir of culture, idioms come and go: they are born, live for a while, age and die. New expressions are being created today, that enjoy a moment of fame, but soon disappear as fast as they came (eg., the slide from *swell --> neat, groovy --> cool --> awesome*, etc.) Some idioms, however, do survive to become a part of the tradition for a while, and eventually will phase out. Only a few stand the test of time.

It is hoped that many of the idioms presented in this book belong to that last traditional, surviving category.

Organization of the materials

The book contents are divided into two sections:

1. The first section is presented from the perspective of a speaker of English asking repeatedly this one question: *"How do you say... in French"*/« *Comment dit-on... en français* ». The equivalent is then immediately provided, along with explanations and origins for both the English and French idioms.

Example: *Comment dit-on...*

"To put the cart before the horse."
– It relates to a mode of transportation.

« *Mettre la charrue avant les bœufs* »
– It refers to the experience of an agrarian society. While a *horse* evokes friskiness and speed, the word *oxen* evokes the slow and steady strength needed to *plow* the ground.

2. The second section places the English speaker in the position of a listener, a situation at least as frequent as the previous perspective. The question then is: *"What do you understand?" Que comprenez-vous?...* This kind of practice (known in pedagogy as the skills of *listening comprehension* and *reading*) is essential, insofar as native speakers of any language are not always aware of the *idiomatic status* of the expressions they are using when addressing speakers of another language. For this reason, they cannot always tailor their level of language to a foreign listener's language competence.

Example: **We hear**/*Nous entendons...* (in a situation of someone describing his relationship with a person):

« *Je me suis mis en quatre pour elle!* » The expression *Se mettre en quatre* means to fold one's body into four parts. The idea of help and personal sacrifice in a given context should suggest an English equivalent, such as ***"bending over backward"/"going the extra mile"/"going out of one's way."*** At any rate, roughly discerning the meaning of the expression « ***se mettre en quatre pour…*** » is already an accomplishment; finding the proper equivalent is a victory!

PART ONE

Jacques Bourgeacq

ENGLISH IDIOMS

Why do we use images, similes and metaphors to communicate our thoughts? Just as it is with the statement on spirituality: *"man does not live on bread alone"* (Deuteronomy), we humans also possess a basic, innate urge to comprehend the world and our relation to it. It may be a deep, unconscious philosophical search for unity. Among our basic mental functions are comparing and contrasting, that is, to view and express parallel processes between different realms of reality. For example, if I say as in an old French song: « *Mon cœur est un violon, sur lequel ton archet joue...* » (un archet is a bow), I establish a connection between human reciprocal love and musical experience. I am basically saying: *love is like music to my soul.* This comparison has several effects: It produces in the listener an instantaneous surprise and an increase of attention. Along with our sensorial imagination, the reasoning and emotional functions have been triggered. This explains why poets would not be poets without similes and metaphors, which they must constantly create anew for a more striking effect on our imagination.

I. Selection of similes in English and French

Comparative and contrasting thinking is an essential part of how we relate to the world, and using images is a way of illuminating our abstract thoughts. Every culture has invented idioms centered on the various realms of our physical environment: the animal world, parts of the human body, familiar objects surrounding us, and in fact numerous areas of our lives, as we shall see in the pages ahead.

Similes of adjectives: (Note the frequent images of animals)

Brave as a lion — *courageux comme un lion*

Busy as a bee (beaver) — *occupé comme jamais (s'affairer comme une fourmi)*

Clean as a whistle — *propre comme un sou neuf*
– A whistle must be clean to produce a clear sound. And a brand-new penny (*un sou neuf*) is cleaner than an old one.

Dead as a dodo — *mort et enterré*

Easy as pie — *simple comme bonjour*
– Refers to the eating, not the making, of a pie. *It's a piece of cake* has a similar connotation. Bonjour is the easier thing to say as a greeting.

Fit as a fiddle — *en pleine forme/se porter comme un charme*
– Musical instruments must be kept in perfect condition to be fit for playing. Regarding the French expression *se porter comme un charme*, in the 12th century, **un charme** (from the Latin *carmen*, meaning chant, incantation) meant a talisman, supposed to bring good luck to whoever wore it. **Se porter** is apparently a pun: *se porter* means to be worn; and **se porter bien** or **mal** means to be in

good or bad health.

Free as a bird	*libre comme l'air*
Happy as a lark	*heureux comme un poisson dans l'eau*

– The beautiful song of this bird evokes happiness.

(To be) hungry as a bear	*(avoir) une faim de loup*
Meek as a lamb	*doux comme un agneau*
As mute as a fish	*muet comme une carpe*
Pretty as a picture	*joli(e) comme un cœur*

– The word *picture* stood for beautiful objects from the 18th century on; in French *un cœur* is pretty if it is presented as a colorful picture…

Proud as a peacock	*fier comme un coq*

– The appearance and behavior of both animals evoke pride.

Red as a lobster	*rouge comme une écrevisse (sunburn)/comme une tomate (emotion)*
Ugly as sin	*laid/moche/comme un pou*

– Obviously, sin evokes ugliness. But in French, why *un pou* (a louse)? In late 18th century, the already existing microscope allowed a clear view of an insect whose frequent infestation made it even more repulsive!

Wise as an owl	*sage comme un vieux hibou (sage comme une image)*

– From antiquity (India and Greece) the owl has been a symbol of wisdom. By its nocturnal vigilance, the owl was associated with Athena, the Greek and wise goddess of darkness.

A guide for the exercises
Research strategy for completing the exercises

Using the internet and/or bilingual anthologies of idioms, you will be able to research and select the proper idioms in French. Based on the author's and the editors' own experience with the internet, we recommend the method below for completing the exercises in this section.

First, using your favorite search engine (*Google, Yahoo,* etc.) enter the idiom whose equivalent you wish to find, followed by the word **traduction** or **translation**, as the case may be. The results will show several sites to choose from (*linguee, reverso, fr.bab.la,* etc.) Through validation and practice, you will soon discover which sites are more reliable and easier to use for the purposes of these exercises.

For the process of validation, that is, to ensure you are actually seeing an idiom in use and not machine translation, you may wish to compare the results found in several sites. You will then enter the most commonly-found equivalents between quotes on a search engine and choose the equivalent with the most hits in its original language. For example:

Strong as an ox traduction renders over 61,000 results in Google.

Linguee will be at the top of the results: *fort comme un bœuf.*

Reverso will follow with *fort comme un Turc.*

fr.bab.la shows *fort comme un bœuf.* That's already two results with the same equivalent.

You would then enter in the search engine the most commonly found equivalent using quote marks (this is called a Boolean search, to narrow down results to an exact set of words): « fort comme un *bœuf* » renders almost 57,000 matches. « fort comme un Turc » renders a little over 30,000 matches. This validates « fort comme un *bœuf* » as the most commonly used equivalent for "*strong as an ox.*"

Another way of validating the equivalent found is to conduct a reverse search: enter the idiom you have found accompanied by the word *translation* or *traduction*, and see if you get back your original idiom.

A definite advantage of search engines is that idioms are often presented in various contexts.

To research the origin of an idiom, type the word **origine** or **origin** next to the idiom you have entered. Expect to obtain varying results. The context in which you wish to use your idiom will ultimately help select the most appropriate equivalent.

Note: Learning and comparing the origin of idioms, in your own language and in the foreign language, can add a cultural dimension to your search we strongly recommend. It also helps, through mental association, to remember the idioms you research.

Exercise: Research and provide equivalent idioms in French for the following:

1. Poor as a church mouse _____

2. Talkative as a magpie/a chatterbox _____

3. Dumb as a post _____

4. I am sick as a dog _____

5. He is skinny as a rail _____

6. He is sly (cunning) as a fox _____

7. This prof is stubborn as a mule _____

8. (From the flu) She was pale as a ghost _____

9. I am stone-deaf/deaf as a post _____

10. He was solemn as a judge _____

II. English idioms using names of animals

Observing the animal world in its behavior has produced in our western cultures many images and symbols applicable by association to the human experience. Oral and written tales and fables, as well as sayings and proverbs, are found around the world (e.g. in Asia, in Africa, etc. depicting animals as substitutes or partners to human protagonists. Aside from these literary devices, animal-related idioms have been coined in all languages through the ages.

1. Birds

To eat like a bird   *avoir un appétit d'oiseau*
- This generally means to eat very little, which is a case where observation was faulty, since in reality birds eat much more than humans proportional to size!

A bird-brain   *une cervelle d'oiseau*
- *Cervelle* is used for animals, while *cerveau* is for humans, except for a negative connotation.

A bird's eye view   *une vue d'ensemble/une vue aérienne*
- *Un ensemble* means a whole, a totality, overall.

A little bird told me.   *C'est mon petit doigt qui me l'a dit.*
- The *petit doigt* is the pinky finger. Why the pinky? Because of its other name *l'auriculaire*, which comes from **auri,** meaning *oreille,* and **culaire,** meaning *cleaner.* The French saying establishes that the ear and the pinky are close confidants.

Learn the birds and the bees   *apprendre les choses de la vie (the facts of life)*

– An euphemistic explanation for children about reproduction, pollination and hatching. The English idiom is attributed to several poets of the 17th to the 19th century, as well as Cole Porter's song "*Let's do it, let's fall in love.*"

A stool pigeon	un mouchard

– Originally, it was a hunting practice to place a pigeon as a decoy on a "***stoal***" (the stump of a tree). Today the meaning has changed. A **stool** pigeon is an informer placed as a "*decoy*" by the police. The French term comes from the Great Inquisition. A well-known informer at the time called **Mouchy** unwillingly gave its name to the whole class of informers, *les mouches* at first, and then *les mouchards*. The suffix **-ard** is often derogatory.

What is good for the goose is good for the gander.	Ce qui est bon pour l'un est bon pour l'autre.

– The 17th century form of this expression was based on culinary experience: "What's **sauce** for the goose is **sauce** for the gander." In other words, they could be prepared (i.e. treated) equally.

A bird in the hand worth two in the bush	Un tiens vaut mieux que deux tu l'auras.

– A medieval falconry expression: The bird here is a falcon held by the hunter, while the two in the bush are mere potential preys. The French *tiens* is an imperative form of *tenir*, uttered while handing over an object to someone. *Tu l'auras* is a mere promise.

All this work for the birds!	*Tout ce travail pour des prunes.*

– Although seemingly unrelated, given the mention of birds, this early 20th century American idiom refers to the droppings left behind horse-drawn carriages. The French version dates back to the failed 2nd Crusade (12th century): the French king allegedly asked if all the crusaders could show as proof of their success was the plumtrees they had brought back home.

Exercise: Research and provide equivalent idioms in French for the following.

Côte à Côte 3

1. Don't count your chickens before they hatch _____

2. A little bird told me _____

3. Birds of a feather flock together _____

4. This is (strictly) for the birds _____

5. The early bird gets the worm _____

6. To hit two birds with one stone _____

7. A distance as the crow flies _____

8. He chickened out! _____

9. The rooster may crow, but this hen lays the egg _____

10. They were all sitting ducks _____

2. Dogs

Dog days (of summer)	*les grandes chaleurs d'été/la canicule*

– Refers to Sirius, the dog star rising with the sun in July-August. La canicule comes from the Latin **canicula**, meaning little female dog.

It's raining cats and dogs.	*Il pleut à torrent/des cordes/à verse/à seaux*

– In olden times, cats and dogs resting in a thatch roof in search of a cool spot would come down from the ceiling when it poured down rain. The first French written mention of « Il pleut à torrent » dates back to the end of the 18th century. **Cordes** (ropes) is an optical illusion.

Can't teach an old dog new tricks.	On est trop vieux pour changer/ On ne fait pas du neuf avec du vieux

To be in the doghouse	*Etre sur la selette/Ne pas être en odeur de sainteté*

– From Barrie's novel <u>Peter Pan</u>, in which a father punishes himself by putting himself in a kennel for having allowed his children to be kidnapped. Today it is someone angry who puts you "*in the doghouse.*" For the French version, **une selette** was long ago a low witness seat used in courts, so that judges could "*dominate*" the situation and thus intimidate more easily. For the second French example, there was once a belief that saints produced a special pleasant scent... The reverse was to be logically expected for one who did not act in a saintly manner. Isn't the devil associated with sulphur?

A doggy bag	*un sac à emporter*

– A doggy bag is very much an American idiom. Though the practice is rare in France, the notion of taking home an order of food exists, just not the leftover from a meal in a restaurant.

Exercise: Research and provide equivalent idioms in French.

1. Barking dogs seldom bite _____

2. To fight like cats and dogs _____

3. It's a dog's life _____

4. It's the tail wagging the dog _____

5. It's a dog-eat-dog world _____

6. He is barking up the wrong tree _____

3. Cats

A copycat	*un copieur (une copieuse)/un imitateur/un singe*
Curiosity killed the cat.	*La curiosité est un vilain défaut.*

– For an animal with *"nine lives,"* curiosity must be a dangerous threat.

Let sleeping cats (dogs) lie.	*Il ne faut pas réveiller le chien qui dort/Ne revenons pas là-dessus*

– This written image in English dates back to Chaucer. For the French, ***ne pas revenir là-dessus*** means to skip something.

Looks like the cat that swallowed the canary.	*On dirait un chat qui vient d'avaler un canari.*

– Note **the** canary, not just any canary, i.e. the other pet of the house. (This implies a hint of guilt mixed with some discrete satisfaction!)

Pussyfooting around	*tergiverser/tourner autour du pot*

– As in the cautious gait of a cat. The expression was used in the early 20th century to describe the delay tactics of Indian Affairs agents in their deceitful dealing with the Native Americans. The French turn around **the pot**, not around the bush...

A scaredy-cat	*un peureux/un trouillard/un froussard*

– For the French, **la trouille** and **la frousse** have to do with the lower-track digestive functions! And the suffix **--ard** has a derogatory connotation.

The cat is out of the bag.	*On a vendu la mèche.*

– For the French, the word ***mèche*** here means a wick used for triggering an explosion. ***Vendre*** stands for exposing, as a wick suggests the presence of explosives inside a mine.

It's no big deal!	*Il n'y a pas de quoi fouetter un chat!*

– Why a cat in the French saying? The expression may allude to the ***cat of nine tails***, a whip originally used in the Navy as an instrument of punishment. This is pure supposition, but it would make sense...

Exercise: Research and provide equivalent idioms in French.

1. An alley cat _____

2. All cats are gray in the dark _____

3. To take a cat nap _____

4. To play cat and mouse _____

5. When the cat is away, mice will play_____
   _____

6. A sourpuss _____

There is more than one way to skin a cat _____

4. Fish

He is a big fish in a small pond   *Au royaume des aveugles les borgnes sont rois.*
- The French idiom dates back to ancient Greece, and was used in the 16th century by Erasmus. **Un borgne** is a one-eyed person.

There are other fish in the sea.   *Un(e) de perdu(e), dix de retrouvé(e)s*
- Both of these expressions are often used as a consolation after the end of a love relationship.

(for a person) a cold fish   *un pisse-froid*

There is something fishy.   *Il y a du louche/quelque chose de louche/il y a anguille sous roche*
- What is slimy and smelly cannot be very safe. In the French, **une anguille** (an eel) specifically, is slimy. **Sous roche** means hidden. **Louche** is the word for *shady, suspect*.

Holy Mackerel!   *Ça alors!/C'est le bouquet!*
- An old euphemism of **Holy Mary!** or **Holy Moses! Ça alors!** is a speechless reaction. **Le bouquet** describes the grand finale of a fireworks display. It is used here ironically.

Exercise: Research and provide equivalent idioms in French.

1. I have bigger fish to fry _____

2. To drink like a fish _____

3. To feed the fish (sea sickness) _____

4. To be like a fish out of water _____

5. He is a big fish! (a person) _____

5. Horses

Hold your horses!   *Minute!/Il n'y a pas le feu!*

It's a horse of a different color.   *C'est une autre paire de manches.*
– The English idiom dates back to the Middle Ages: Horses were clad during tournaments to identify the knights in their armors. In 16th century France, **sleeves** (*manches*) were sewn temporarily and changed for different tasks or occasions).

Straight from the horse's mouth   *de source sûre/à la source*
– The teeth of a horse was thought to be a surer sign of its health than the words of a trader!

To be (get) on one's high horse   *monter sur ses grands chevaux*
– A high horse is thought to be more powerful, and the rider in a dominating and haughty position.

Horse trading   *du marchandage/du maquignonnage (pej.)*
– Honesty has not been the hallmark of horse traders. For the French, **marchander** means to haggle. **Un maquignon** is a horse trader and **maquignonnage** is applied to all sorts of deceptive dealings.

You can bring a horse to water,   *On ne fait pas boire un âne*
but you can't make it drink.   *qui n'a pas soif.*
– The French speaks of a donkey instead of a horse… When it comes to stupidity, the French seem less forgiving!

Horseplay is not allowed in school.	*Le chahut n'est pas permis à l'école.*

– In 16th century England, ***horse*** was also an adjective meaning strong and rough. ***Un chahut*** was originally a 19th century disorderly dance whose meaning later changed to *uproar* and *perturbation*.

<u>Exercise</u>: Research and provide equivalent idioms in French.

1. A charley horse _____

2. To beat a dead horse _____

3. Trojan horse _____

4. I could eat a horse. _____

5. To put the cart before the horse _____

6. Quit horsing around! _____

7. Get off your high horse! _____

6. Cows and bulls

Until the cows come home	*Quand les poules auront des dents.*

– Presumably, unlike horses, escaped cows don't seem to return to the barn on their own...

Like a bull in a china shop	*Comme un chien dans un jeu de quilles*

– Origin unknown; found in 19th century literature. For the French, ***quilles*** are bowling pins.

Holy cow! (a euphemism)	*Oh, la vache!*

– Uncertain origin; may be a reference to the biblical golden calf. Or perhaps a euphemism for the Virgin Mary.

A cash cow	*une vache à lait/une poule aux œufs d'or*

– Another name for **dairy** cow. Metaphorically referring to a business generating a steady income with low investment.

That's a lot of bull!	*C'est des conneries, tout ça!*

– **Bull** may have been derived from old French **boul**, meaning fraud, deceipt. **Bull** is now a euphemism for *bullshit*, often abbreviated as BS. For the French, **connerie** has lost its original reference to female genitals, to now mean *nonsensical talk or action*.

Exercise: Research and provide equivalent idioms in French.

1. A sacred cow (pej.) _____

2. To take the bull by the horns _____

3. Until the cows come home _____

4. To hit the bull's eye _____

5. The golden calf _____

7. Pigs

To go all hog	*se donner à fond/ s'investir corps et âme*

– Probably an 18th century expression aimed at Islam's pork taboo. Attributed to English poet William Cowper: *"Mahometans eat up the hog."* For the French, **à fond** means *completely*.

If pigs had wings...	*Avec des si, on mettrait Paris en bouteille.*

– The English idiom appears to come from the 16th century. Both expressions stress wishful thinking.

Put lipstick on a pig, it's still a pig	*Faire prendre des vessies pour des lanternes.*

- Idioms with pigs were used throughout the Middle Ages, but apparently lipstick was not invented till the end of the 19th century. In the Middle Ages, pork bladders (**vessies**) could be confused as lamps. But, empty of candles, they were not lanterns!

A piggy bank	*une tirelire*

- Medieval pots, pink in color, were used to store money: "*piggy jar,*" later called "*piggy banks.*"

- For the French, **tirelire** may come from the Italian **tira lira,** meaning *drawing* this currency.

Riding piggyback	*monter à califourchon*

- Obscure origin. May be a corruption of "*pickaback*" or "*pick a pack,*" that is carried on the back. **Califourchon** may come from old Celtic "**cale**" *(crotch)* and French **fourche** *(pitchfork).* Perhaps in contrast with Victorian side-saddle mounting.

<u>Exercise</u>: Research and provide equivalent idioms in French.

1. To serve as a guinea pig _____

2. To sweat like a pig _____

3. To pig out _____

4. To eat like a pig _____

5. To make a pig of oneself _____

8. Monkeys

Can't teach a monkey how to grin.	*On n'apprend pas à un vieux singe à faire la grimace.*

To go ape   *péter les plombs/s'emballer*
- To show wild excitement, as a monkey often does. **Péter les plombs** is a synonym of "**to blow a fuse**," referring to the fuse box in a house. **S'emballer** means to run wild like a runaway horse.

Monkey business   *une affaire louche/des manigances*
- Probably coined after a Bengali idiom with similar meaning. For the French, the adjective **louche** means shady and **manigances** is *a scheme*.

To make a monkey of someone   *tourner quelqu'un en ridicule*
- A medieval expression, found in <u>Roman de Renard</u>, where the character named *Moneke* is a monkey. A monkey is viewed as often showing erratic behavior.

Don't monkey around   *Ne fais pas l'idiot/Ne fais pas de conneries*
- For the French, **Faire l'idiot** means **acting like an idiot**. **Une connerie** with the verb **faire** means to **make** a stupid mistake.

More fun than   *marrant comme tout!*
a barrel of monkeys
- Originally, this mid-19th century idiom was "*a cage full of monkeys*," presumably a funny spectacle.

- For the French, **marrant** means **amusant**; the expression **comme tout** corresponds to **ever so** plus an adjective.

I got the monkey off my back   *Je suis soulagé d'un poids.*
- Probably a 16th century low German idiom. A monkey knows how to grab, so does a persistent problem. For the French, **soulager** means **to relieve**.

<u>Exercise</u>: Research and provide equivalent idioms in French.

1. Monkey see monkey do _____

2. To ape someone _____

3. I'll be a monkeys' uncle! _____

4. A monkey wrench _____

9. Rats

A rat race   *une foire d'empoigne*
– Either the image of laboratory maze, whereby rats run to get to the cheese, or an early aviation expression describing pilots sticking to a leader throughout aerobatic maneuvers. For the French, from the verb ***empoigner***, meaning to grab.

To smell a rat   *soupçonner quelque chose de louche*
– It appeared in 17th century Samuel Johnson's dictionary: to smell a rat, as a cat would. For the French, ***louche*** means shady, suspect.

To rat on someone   *dénoncer/moucharder quelqu'un*
– ***A rat*** is a metaphor for an informer. ***To rat on*** is to denounce, turn in someone or something.

You dirty rat!   *Sale mouchard!*
– An expression made famous by actor James Cagney in a 1932 film, *Taxi!*

Exercise: Research and provide equivalent idioms in French.

1. A rat hole (lodging) _____

2. A rat pack (U.S. artists) _____

3. Mall rats _____

4. A rat trap (situation) _____

10. Wild animals

The expressions listed in this section are identical in meaning in both languages.

To cry wolf	*crier au loup*

– From a well-known Aesop's fable.

A lone wolf	*un loup solitaire*

– Unlike other wolves that are pack animals.

A wolf in sheep's clothing	*un loup déguisé en agneau*

– Of Aesop and biblical origins. It is also found in Matthew's gospel, describing false prophets.

To get the lion's share	*avoir la part du lion*

– Attributed to Aesop.

To have a tiger by its tail	*tenir un tigre par la queue*

– Seems like a catch-22 situation! The expression may have originated in India at the time of British rule. Guess who the lion may have been...

To throw in the lion's den	*jeter dans la fosse aux lions*

– May refer to Nero's persecution of Christians.

A paper tiger	*un tigre de papier*

– A literal translation from Chinese and its paper-cutting art, **jianzhi**. A paper tiger (e.g., an image for a powerless country) presents little danger.

Exercise: Research and provide equivalent idioms in French.

1. Throw (someone) to the wolves _____

2. A leopard can't change its spots _____

3. To weasel out of (something) _____

4. A wild-goose chase _____

11. Insects

To have a bee in your bonnet   *avoir une idée en tête/une idée fixe*
- The English is actually from a 16th century Scottish expression, meaning an obsession, to say the least!

To make a bee-line   *se diriger tout droit*
- In English, wild bees are said to fly in a straight line.

Bitten by the travel bug   *avoir le virus des voyages*
- In both languages, though positive in meaning, an obsessive desire to travel is linked metaphorically to an infecting bug. The expression can be used for any strong interest, such as the soccer bug, the gardening bug, etc.

To put a bug in someone's ear   *mettre la puce à l'oreille à...*
- In medieval times, societies suffered all sorts of insect infestations. A flea in one's ear seems to have indicated a situation that required some urgent action... For the French, **to put** or **mettre** (to place) a **flea** (not just any bug) in someone's ear seems to serve as a most urgent warning.

To have butterflies   *avoir le trac/la gorge nouée*
in one's stomach
- Refers to a fluttery sensation one feels in the stomach when anxious or anguished. The French middle 19th century expression's origin is uncertain: **Le trac** may be derived from the French word **tracas**, meaning anguish, anxiety.

To have ants in one's pants   *avoir la bougeotte/*
    ne pas tenir en place
- Anyone who ever stepped on an ant-hill (especially fireants!) knows the difficulty of standing still.

Bug off/out!   *Dégage! Du vent!*
- The French **dégager** means to make space; **du vent** refers to the air displaced by a body's movement.

Don't bug me!   *Lâche-moi le coude!*
- The French means let go of my elbow; in other words: *Let me go.*

The flea market — *le marché aux puces*
– A mid-19th century French idiom describing a used goods market, probably with some clothing likely to harbor fleas!

Exercise: Research and provide equivalent idioms in French.

1. He would not hurt a flea (fly) _____

2. To be busy as a bee _____

3. Don't let the bed bugs bite _____

4. To be snug as a bug _____

5. A beehive of activity _____

6. A hornet's nest _____

12. Other animals

The elephant in the room — *l'éléphant dans la pièce/le gros tabou/le point noir*
– This English saying dates back to a 19th century fable by Ivan Andrevich Krylov, "*The Inquisitive Man,*" who does not see an actual elephant roaming in a museum.

To have bats in the belfry — *avoir des araignées au plafond*
– An early 19th century English expression in America: Ideas, like bats in a church steeple, can fly erratically in the head.

A kangaroo court — *un tribunal fantoche*
– This English saying was probably coined during the Gold Rush, when courts accepted claims from place to place. The courts were effectively jumping from place to place, like this animal. In the French expression, *fantoche* comes from the Italian *fantoccio*, which means puppet.

The straw that broke the camel's back	*la goutte d'eau qui a fait déborder le vase*

– The English apparently comes from an Arab proverb or story.

The black sheep (of a group)	*la brebis galeuse (le mouton noir)*

– Like many natural oddities, a black sheep was once viewed as a bad omen, if not as a sign of the devil. For the French, ***galeuse*** means mangy, scabious, believed to be infectious.

Bright-eyed and bushy-tailed	*frais et dispos/tout pimpant*

– Probably from Rudyard Kipling' The Jungle book, a story of a mangoose and a cobra. For the French, ***pimpant*** is a synonym of *elegant, stylish*.

Exercise: Research and provide equivalent idioms in French.

1. To make a mountain out of a molehill _____
   _____

2. An eager beaver _____

3. The lost sheep _____

4. To have a whale (hell) of a time _____

5. To squirrel away (sth) _____

III. English idioms using body parts

Our body is obviously the closest part of the "*environment*" that we relate to. The abundance of images of parts of the human body used in idioms should come as no surprise. This is the case for both English and French, though not always in unison, and with the same meaning.

1. Arm:

Twist my arm (about a drink)   *C'est bien pour te faire plaisir.*

It costs an arm and a leg.   *Cela coûte les yeux de la tête/la peau des fesses.*

– Values of body parts can differ from culture to culture, as does sometimes the level of language!

It was a shot in the arm.   *Cela m'a donné un coup de fouet.*
– With a stimulating drug for energy. For the French, the lash of a whip can have a similar effect.

Exercise: Research and provide equivalent idioms in French.

1. At arm's length _____

2. I'd give my right arm for... _____

3. To receive with open arms _____

4. The long arm of the law _____

2. Back:

I break my back (for my firm).   *Je me coupe en quatre pour...*
– *Se couper en quatre* is an image of self-sacrifice, just like **breaking** one's back.

Get off my back.   *Fiche-moi la paix.*
– Presumably as removing a load. For the French, the verb *ficher* (from the Latin *figere*) means to insert. It is often a euphemism for the sexual verb *foutre* (*la paix*).

You scratch my back   *Un service en vaut*
and I'll scratch yours.   *un autre.*
– This idiom originated in the 17th century British Navy, when punishment was flogging. Deals were made between sailors for the flogging to be "*light*," hence the "*scratching*" of the whip. At any rate, scratching your own back requires a bit of effort and flexibility!

To have one's back to the wall   *être le dos au mur/être coincé*
– Unable to retreat farther. For the French, **coincer** (from **un coin**, meaning a corner).

Exercise: Research and provide equivalent idioms in French.

1. Don't talk behind my back _____

2. I've got your back _____

3. I have my back against the wall _____

4. They stabbed me in the back _____

3. Belly:

A beer (pot) belly   *une panse de buveur de bière*

A belly laugh   *un gros rire*

The firm went belly-up.	*La compagnie a coulé.*

– Probably like a dying fish or another animal.

A yellow-belly	*un trouillard*

– Originated in 18th century England, without the idea of cowardice. In 19th century America, it acquired that connotation in the war against Mexicans (called Yellow-bellies). Another theory is that the liver, once considered the seat of courage, is the organ that can cause yellow jaundice, and discoloration of the skin and eyes.

– « *Avoir les foies* » (to have livers) means to be afraid. **La trouille** means diarrhea. **Un trouillard** is a coward.

Exercise: Research and provide equivalent idioms in French.

1. A belly flop (swimming) _____

2. I've my bellyful of it _____

4. Bones:

To make no bones about it	*Dire les choses comme elles sont/*
	Ne pas y aller de main morte/
	Ne pas y aller par quatre chemins

– A 15th century England expression, supposedly related to making soup easier to eat without bones in it.

– The French comes from a 17th century expression: « *ne pas toucher de main morte.* » **Une main morte** is an inactive, insensitive hand. The opposite (ne pas) indicates strength and even violence. It can be physical or psychological. **Par quatre chemins** would be the opposite of *directly*.

To have a bone to pick with...	*avoir un compte à régler avec/*
	avoir maille à partir avec

– An old image which changed meaning in the early 19th century from an issue to be solved to a dispute between two people. **Une maille** was a medieval coin, the smallest and of worthless value. Back then, *partir* did not meant to depart, but to split, to divide. So dividing a worthless coin was not only impossible, but led to quarrels!

A bone of contention *une pomme de discorde/un sujet de discorde/de désaccord/une pierre d'achoppement*

– A 16th century English idiom alluding to a couple of dogs competing for one bone. The French comes from the 17th century verb **achopper**, meaning to hit an obstacle.

A budget cut down to the bone *un budget réduit au strict minimum*

This dish will stick to my ribs. *Ce plat me tiendra au ventre.*

A skeleton in (someone's) closet *un cadavre/un squelette dans le placard*

– A metaphor originated in the English Romantic era, when skeletons were fashionable in literature and were hidden in secret places such as a closet or a cupboard.

Exercise: Research and provide equivalent idioms in French.

1. He is a bag of bones_____

2. This river is bone dry _____

3. This pottery is bone dry _____

4. Chilled to the bones _____

5. I know in my bones that... _____

5. Brain:

The brain drain *l'exode des cerveaux*

May I pick your brain? *Puis-je faire appel à vos lumières?*

He is a scatter-brain.   *C'est un écervelé.*

To rack your brain   *se creuser la tête*
- From **a rack**, a medieval device of torture. The verb is found in Shakespeare's *Twelfth Night*.

- **Creuser** means to dig.

(Someone's) brainchild   *l'invention de.../l'idée personnelle de...*
- The English apparently originated in the mid-19th century.

Exercise: Research and provide equivalent idioms in French.

1. Brain-dead _____

2. To be a bird-brain _____

3. This is a no-brainer! _____

4. We had a brainstorm _____

6. Chin:

Take it on the chin   *Encaisse bravement*
- A boxing term applied to life experience. For the French, **encaisser**, of uncertain origin, here means to *absorb* a blow, or criticism by extension.

Keep your chin up.   *Gardez la tête haute./Tenez bon.*
- A late 19th century American idiom, and the opposite of lowering one's head. For the French, **tenir bon**, meaning *to hold tight*. **Bon** is used here as an adverb.

7. Ears:

I am all ears.   *Je suis tout oreilles./tout ouïe.*
- For the French, **l'ouïe** is the sense of hearing.

To play by ear (music) *jouer d'oreille*
- To play from memory, as opposed to a music score.

Play it by ear (figurative) *Improvisez, le moment venu.*
- Metaphorically, this idiom adapts to different contexts, meaning *to act without any specific plan.*

He is wet behind the ears. *Il est né de la dernière pluie./de la dernière couvée.*
- An early 20th century American idiom: Like a new-born baby out of the womb, i.e. without any experience. The French idiom refers to newly **hatched** chicks (**une couvée** is a *brood*).

It's music to my ears. *Ça me fait chaud au cœur.*

Exercise: Research and provide equivalent idioms in French.

1. It gets in one ear and out in the other _____

2. It didn't fall on deaf ears _____

3. Smoke was coming out of his ears _____

4. Walls have ears! _____

5. He was bending my ears _____

8. Eyes:

Keep an eye on the child. *Gardez un œil sur cet enfant.*

We see eye to eye. *Nous sommes d'accord/du même avis*
- This saying is as old as the Bible.

to turn a blind eye on... *fermer les yeux sur...*
- A legend puts the origin of this expression on Admiral Nelson, who

had actually lost an eye in battle. He is said to have disobeyed an order, blaming it on his half-blindness!

It was an eye-opener.   *Ça m'a ouvert les yeux.*
– An American idiom, synonym of an enlightening experience.

An eye for an eye   *Œil pour œil, dent pour dent.*
and a tooth for a tooth.
– An ancient expression dating all the way back to Mesopotamian culture.

I can't focus   *Je n'ai pas les yeux en face des trous.*
– **Un trou** (a hole) here means an orbit.

Exercise: Research and provide equivalent idioms in French.

1. With the naked eye _____

2. In the wink of an eye _____

3. A black eye _____

4. To catch someone's eye _____

5. I have an eye on this car _____

6. They have an eye on this suspect _____

9. Fingers:

Cross your fingers.   *Croisez les doigts/Faites un vœu/ Touchez du bois*
– A religious gesture, forming a cross, invented by the early Christians to ask for God's protection in times of persecution. **Knock on wood** is an alternate idiom to express the same idea.

He didn't lift a finger.   *Il n'a même pas levé le petit doigt.*

A butter-fingers   *un maladroit/un empoté*
- **Empoté** is from **pote** (gauche) and possibly old Celtic **pauta** (patte).

Under someone's thumb   *sous la coupe de (qqn)/sous la domination de*
- An 18th century idiom, meaning to be under someone's total control, as if a thumb were sufficient to immobilize a person. The French coupe may have originated from *"cutting"* the deck in a card game, which determines the distribution of cards.

Exercise: Research and provide equivalent idioms in French.

1. He has a finger in every pie _____

2. Do not point your finger _____

3. To thumb one's nose _____

4. To have (someone) wrapped around your finger _____
_____

10. Feet:

To drag your feet   *traîner les pieds/Faire traîner les choses*
- A person drags his feet when *his heart is not in it*!

To put your best foot forward   *se montrer à son avantage*

To put your feet up   *se détendre/se requinquer*
- With feet up, one does not move away and can thus relax. **Requinquer** is an old verb meaning to repair, spruce up. **La quincaillerie** (hardware) may have the same root.

To put your foot down   *mettre le holà/taper du point*
- Putting a foot on the ground is creating a firm support, as digging one's heels in. For the French, **Holà!** is an exclamation meaning to stop.

He put his foot in his mouth	*Il a perdu une belle occasion de se taire/Il a mis les pieds dans le plat/ Il a gaffé*

– This may come from a 19th century name of a virus affecting cattle: foot-and-mouth disease.

He always put his foot in it.	*Il n'en rate pas une.*

– The French expression speaks about **une** what? It suggests a blunder, a gaffe. Ironically put, he never misses such an opportunity to make a gaffe! **Rater** means manquer.

To shoot oneself in the foot	*se tirer une balle dans le pied/se faire du tort*

– This expression may have originated from a strategy used by some WWI soldiers who shot themselves in the foot in the trenches to be removed from battle.

He got cold feet	*Il s'est dégonflé/a fait marche arrière*

– For whatever reason, cold feet make it difficult to move ahead. For the French expression, **se dégonfler** means to **deflate**, an image for a loss of enthusiasm. **Faire marche arrière** is a term used in driving: to back up.

To pull the rug from under someone's feet	*Lui couper l'herbe sous les pieds*

– In olden times, growing grass was a way of subsistence in an agrarian society. Cutting it under someone's feet was destroying his chances of survival.

To foot the bill	*payer la note/la facture/l'addition*

– A 19th century accounting expression: the total of a bill being at the "*foot*" of an invoice, **footing the bill** has evolved to mean paying for it.

Exercise: Research and provide equivalent idioms in French.

1. He has two left feet _____

2. My foot! _____

3. Get a foot in the door _____

4. From head to toe _____

5. To get off on the wrong foot _____

11. Hair:

He gets in my hair.   *Il me tape sur les nerfs.*
– A persistent annoyance rather than a physical pain.

I am pulling my hair out.   *Je m'arrache les cheveux.*
– A compulsive gesture of exasperation or anguish.

To split hairs   *couper les cheveux en quatre*
– Note the precision: **en quatre**, meaning into four parts, lengthwise of course!

Exercise: Research and provide equivalent idioms in French.

1. Escape by a hair's breadth _____

2. To make your hair stand on end _____

3. I am gonna get out of your hair _____

4. Hair-raising news _____

12. Hands:

He is an old hand.   *C'est un vieux briscard/un vieux de la vieille.*
– The combination of **old** and **hand** means experience. For the French, a **briscard** is an old veteran in the 18th century. **Vieux de la vieille** refers to the Old Guard of Napoleon. A **brisque** is a chevron or insignia worn by ranked soldiers.

To have the upper hand	*avoir le dessus/avoir la main sur...*

– Apparently **hand** can be a symbol of control, of superiority.

To catch someone red-handed	*prendre quelqu'un la main dans le sac*

– A 16th century Scottish idiom, probably originating in blood-stain on a murderer's or a poacher's hand.

To get out of hand	*devenir incontrôlable/dégénérer*
A second-hand book	*un livre d'occasion*

– For the French, **occasion** comes from the Latin **ob** *(due to)* and **cadere** *(to fall, occur)*. **Occasion** is a synonym of opportunity, and here the opportunity is to acquire it.

A hand-to-hand combat	*un combat corps à corps/un combat singulier*

– The idea is close contact, and one on one. Perhaps this type of combat did not originally involve weapons.

Exercise: Research and provide equivalent idioms in French.

1. Give me a hand _____

2. My hands are tied _____

3. On the one hand... on the other hand..._____
_____

4. She has a free hand in this _____

5. To hear (get) it first-hand _____

13. Head:

To have a head start	*avoir une longueur d'avance (sur)...*

– As when a horse has a head advantage over other horses at the start of a race.

I am way over my head.	*Je ne suis pas à la hauteur/Je suis dépassé par les événements.*

– Probably originated in an era when many people did not learn to swim. For the French, **pas à la hauteur** corresponds to the English idiom "*not up to the task.*"

He always keeps his head.	*Il garde toujours son calme/son sang-froid/Il ne perd jamais la tête.*

To be in love head over heels	*être éperdument amoureux/amoureux fou*

– First recorded in the 14th century, this idiom became essentially associated with love in 19th century America. For the French, **éperdument** corresponds to *utterly*.

(Something) turns on its head	*mettre sens dessus-dessous/ chambouler complètement*

– To make a complete reversal in interpretation or action from what was in effect. The French expressions stress as well a loss in the order of things, **topsyturviness**. The French word **sens** means here direction, orientation. **Chambouler** means to perturb, upset, turn upside down.

A head-on collision	*une collision frontale*

– From **front**, meaning forehead.

Can't make heads or tails out of....	*Cela...n'a ni queue ni tête*

– This English idiom is from the domain of coin-minting, related to *flipping a coin*. The origin of the French idiom is uncertain: **tête** and **queue** refer to the logical development of a story or explanation.

Exercise: Research and provide equivalent idioms in French.

1. Hold your head up high _____

2. to have one's head in the clouds _____

3. Success went to his head _____

4. to be heading for disaster _____

5. Success went to his head _____

14. Heart:

Eat your heart out!   *Allez vous (faire) rhabiller (chez Plumeau)!*
- Found in Biblical and ancient Greek writings, describing great anguish, this idiom has evolved into wishing a feeling of jealousy on someone who was viewed as superior. For the French, in early 20th century, **Plumeau** was the name of a second-hand clothing dealer. Telling someone to go buy clothes there after a loss is an insult.

To fight your heart out   *se battre comme un(e) lion(ne)*
- In ancient times (Aristotle), the heart was the seat of emotions and intelligence, and courage was one emotion in particular. A good example of this is a verse in 17th century Corneille's Le Cid: « *Rodrigue as-tu du cœur?* »

To have a heart-to-heart talk   *parler à cœur ouvert*
- An exchange in which feelings are expressed openly, honestly, without reservation.

Cross my heart!   *Ma parole d'honneur!*
- A voluntary oath. The theme moves from religion (crossing) to honor.

To know by heart   *savoir par cœur*
- The heart was also considered the seat of memory in ancient times.

At the heart of the matter   *au cœur du sujet/problème/dans le vif du sujet.*
- The word **heart** has been a synonym of a vital part. In a matter, it is

the basic, central principle. For the French, **le vif** was a 15th century expression, meaning the *living flesh*, essentially the heart.

Exercise: Research and provide equivalent idioms in French.

1. She broke my heart _____

2. My heart is not on it _____

3. To have (sth) at heart _____

4. To have a change of heart _____

5. To take to heart _____

6. To be young at heart _____

15. Legs:

You are pulling my leg.   *Tu me fais marcher.*
- An American idiom, whose origin is uncertain. Pulling the leg to trip a person off balance? For the French, **faire marcher** may be putting someone on a wild goose chase?

Break a leg!   *Merde!*
- Vestige of a superstition: A way of wishing good luck before a theater or concert performance, a manner of fooling supernatural evil forces. For the French, **merde!** refers here to horse poop, that 19th century spectators dragged into the theater after stepping out of their horse-drawn carriages. The more poop on the theater rugs, the more spectators, a sign of great success. Strange measuring method!

My car is on its last legs.   *Ma voiture a fait son temps/est au bout de son rouleau.*
- A 16th century expression, whereby **legs** were a metaphor for energy, vitality. Each day bringing a new set of legs, the last one was a sign of near death. Metaphorically, the end of the roll is here the end of the car's *"life."* It will often apply to humans as well. Used for humans,

this idiom was ultimately applied also to things. For the French, *le rouleau* refers to a scroll, ancestor of the book, that had to be unrolled to read the contents.

Do you have sea legs?   *As-tu le pied marin?*
- An old expression dating back to ancient marine, applied to new sailors who had to learn to walk comfortably on a ship at sea.

to have fresh legs   *être d'attaque*
- Describes substitute players put on the field to replace tired teammates. For the French, ***d'attaque*** means in full physical and mental shape.

The first leg of the trip   *le premier tronçon/la première étape du voyage*
- A **"leg"** was at first used metaphorically for ***a ship run on a single tack***, then applied to any distance segment on land. For the French, *tronçon* was a medieval term for a section of a broken lance. Now it is a simple section of a long object, and metaphorically a section of a trip.

Exercise: Research and provide equivalent idioms in French.

1. to stretch your legs _____

2. with his tail between its legs _____

3. This wine has legs (body) _____

4. I'll stretch my legs _____

16. Mouth:

He is (has) a big mouth.   *C'est une grande gueule.*
- ***Une gueule*** is the mouth of an animal. It is derogatory when applied to humans.

He was foaming at the mouth.   *Il était en transes/écumait de rage.*

– A dog with rabies foams at the mouth. In fact, *rabies* is **la rage** in French, which also means *anger* in English.

To live from hand to mouth   *vivre au jour le jour*
– The origin is a 16th century famine in England: Food in the hand went directly to the mouth. No saving for rainy days! The French means *each day at a time*.

Put your money   *Joignez le geste à la parole*
where your mouth is.
– An Irish or American expression originated in the early 20th century. The circumstances are uncertain.

Don't put words in my mouth.   Ne me faites pas dire ce que je n'ai pas dit.

By word of mouth   de bouche à oreille

To pay lip service to...   manifester un intérêt de pure forme
– To pretend approval or interest without believing one word or acting accordingly. The idea (biblical) or even the phrasing may be as old as politicians!

To laugh out of the other   *Rire jaune*
side of the mouth
– May refer to the Roman two-faced god Janus, and its Greek mask. For the French, *jaune* may relate to the pale yellow color of a hepatic face.

Exercise: Research and provide equivalent idioms in French.

1. It makes your mouth water _____

2. You took words right of my mouth _____

3. to be all mouth _____

4. to badmouth someone _____

5. the mouth of a river _____

17. Neck:

He breathes down my neck	Il est toujours sur mon dos/ne me laisse pas respirer.

I won't stick my neck out.   Je ne vais pas me mouiller/ prendre de risques.
– In a way, the neck is the Achilles heel of a turtle or a chicken. For the French, **se mouiller,** which means *to get wet,* is a form of risk.

They are neck and neck.   Ils sont (au) coude à coude/ils sont à égalité/ex æquo
– Apparently borrowed from horse racing. **Ex æquo** is a Latin term meaning *in a tie.*

You are a pain in the neck!   Tu es casse-pieds!/Tu es pénible!
– Dating back to the turn of the 20th century, this idiom appears to be a euphemism for another body part! The French idiom **casse-pieds** really means "*to step on,*" "*to crush*" someone's feet.

I am up to my neck (eyeballs) in emails.   *Je suis dans les courriels jusqu'au cou.*

I am breaking my neck for you.   Je me mets en quatre pour toi.
– *Se mettre en quatre*: To fold oneself in four pieces.

Exercise: Research and provide equivalent idioms in French.

1. In debt up to my neck _____

2. He saved his neck _____

3. You will break your neck _____

4. A region of red-necks _____

18. Nerves:

They get on my nerves.   Ils me tapent sur les nerfs.
– The nervous system is a very sensitive part of the body.

What (a) nerve!   *Quel culot! Quel toupet!*
– Since the 16th century, this idiom has been used to react either to a form of courage or arrogance. For the French, **culot**: A 12th century term that described the base of an object, that provides its balance and steadiness. As an image for a person, it is one whose steadiness can be excessive, i.e. brashness. **Etre culotté** is an alternate expression. **A toupet** was a bunch of hair used in the 15th century by Italian *"bravi"* (hired killers), to hide their identity. They obviously had shameless nerve.

He touched a raw nerve.   *Il a touché un point sensible/Il a touché la corde sensible.*
– Possibly an allusion to the sharp pain felt sometimes on the dentist's chair.

He lost his nerve.   *Il a perdu son sang-froid.*
– As someone's blood is said to be *"boiling"* during a strong emotion, **sang-froid** is a sign of composure and self-control.

Exercise: Research and provide equivalent idioms in French.

1. To be a bundle of nerves _____

2. He didn't have the nerve to ask _____

3. I hit a nerve (in my speech) _____

4. This war of nerves never ends _____

19. Nose:

It's no skin off my nose.   *Ce n'est pas mes oignons/Ça m'est égal*
- This idiom may have originated in boxing, where the nose is a vulnerable appendix of the face. For the French, **oignons** here is not the well-known culinary veggie, but a metaphor for *"personal things."* Why? Because in medieval times, the term referred to the anus, a very personal thing indeed! The plural remains unexplained.

To powder your nose   *se refaire une beauté*
(lady talk)
- A euphemism used by ladies to refer to going to the washroom, where a refresh makeup is sometimes applied. For the French, **la beauté** sometimes has to be refreshed.

Don't turn your nose up at...   *Ne faites pas la fine bouche.*
- The expression describes the gesture of taking a distance from what is proposed, a movement upward (as if away from a bad smell), reflecting a sense of superiority. For the French, **une fine bouche** is a term that applies to gourmet taste. It can also be a metaphor for the person: e.g., *Cet homme est une fine bouche.*

Don't be so nosey   *De quoi je me mêle?/Ne sois pas si curieux.*
- When one wishes to look into something, the nose arrives first! As it is with the expression *"to stick one's nose into someone's business."* For the French, **de quoi je me mêle** is a scolding addressed to a child (stylistically in the first person: **Je**) who asked an indiscrete question or states an unsolicited opinion. It can also be addressed to a nosey adult.

To stick one's nose   *Mettre son grain de sel dans une*
in a conversation   *conversation*
- The French idiom derives from a similar Latin expression meaning a contribution. The negative connotation is a mystery. It is not to be confused with the English **to take with a grain of salt**.

They arrived right on the nose.   *Ils sont arrivés pile à l'heure.*
- This English idiom apparently comes from early radio broadcastings:

a director used gestures for timing, and touching the nose meant perfect timing. For the French, ***pile à l'heure: pile,*** from « pile ou face? » (heads or tails?) refers to the reverse side of a coin, that is minted at a fraction of a second.

To brown-nose *faire de la lèche/lécher les bottes/le cul (vulgar)*
- An apparent military expression describing an overzealous soldier's obsequious behavior towards a superior: Where does one stick his nose to reach this color? The French equivalent is even more explicit, using a different verb: ***lécher***, meaning *to lick*.

<u>Exercise</u>: Research and provide equivalent idioms in French.

1. She leads him by the nose _____

2. To have a nose for (something) _____

3. Can't see further than the tip of your nose _____
_____

4. Follow your nose! _____

5. To thumb your nose at... _____

20. Shoulders:

He gives me the cold shoulder.   *Il me bat froid.*
- Apparently originated in the early 19th century, this expression is related to giving a cold and tough piece of meat to an unwanted guest. The idiom is attributed also to Sir Walter Scott. The French expression dates back to the 15th century (origin unknown), probably alluding to a person's slow heartbeat and cold temperament.

He has a chip on his shoulder.   *Il en veut à tout le monde./Il est aigri.*
- May refer to a 19th century challenge by placing a chip of wood on one's shoulder and daring others to make it fall down. For the

French, the expression *en vouloir à,* *en* probably refers to the idea of grudge, retribution, harm, that someone wishes on whoever has wronged him. *Aigri* means **turned sour.**

He stands head and shoulder above the rest.	*Personne ne lui arrive à la cheville.*

– The height is measured from different angles by each culture, head or ankle.

Exercise: Research and provide equivalent idioms in French.

1. A weight off my shoulders _____

2. I will shoulder my responsibilities. _____

3. To stand shoulder to shoulder (literal) _____ _____

4. To stand shoulder to shoulder (moral) _____ _____

5. To have broad shoulders (moral) _____

21. Skin:

To have a thin skin	*avoir l'épiderme sensible/être susceptible*
To be thick-skinned	*avoir la peau dure/être insensible*
To escape by the skin of your teeth	*échapper de justesse/échapper belle*

– From the Book of Job in the Old Testament: Job is saved from Satan by God at the last minute. **The skin of teeth** is probably an image for a very thin margin. For the French, *de justesse* means barely, narrowly.

He gets under my skin.	*Il m'énerve/il m'exaspère/il m'obsède*

– The literary origin of this idiom is in the 19th century. A superficial rash can be scratched away, but an itch underneath is more unbearable. The idiom is sometimes associated with an irrepressible love.

Beauty is only skin-deep.	*La beauté ne fait pas tout/La beauté est superficielle.*

– Very thin, superficial. Physical beauty, of course.

Exercise: Research and provide equivalent idioms in French.

1. He is skin and bones _____

2. To save one's own skin _____

3. Wet/soaked to the skin _____

22. Stomach:

I have no stomach for this.	*Je n'ai pas l'estomac pour ça.*

– To endure or tolerate, as the stomach does for digestion or indigestion.

This show turned my stomach.	*Ce spectacle m'a retourné l'estomac.*

– The nutritional flow is turned into the other direction.

My eyes were bigger than my stomach/belly	*J'ai eu les yeux plus grands que le ventre.*

– The English describes an overestimated serving.

I cannot stomach him.	*Je ne peux pas le supporter/le blairer/le sentir/le voir en peinture.*

– For the French, **le blair** is a colloquial synonym of **nose**; thus **blairer** means to smell, like **sentir**. It is not about **view**, even if represented in a portrait!

Exercise: Research and provide equivalent idioms in French.

1. On an empty stomach _____

2. Don't sleep on a full stomach _____

3. Butterflies in one's stomach _____

4. Sick to one's stomach _____

23. Teeth:

Armed to the teeth   *armé jusqu'aux dents*
- In an era when guns fired only one bullet at a time, soldiers or pirates had to carry several guns... and for good measure a knife between the teeth.

To fight tooth and nail for...   *défendre... bec et ongles pour...*

I have a sweet tooth.   *J'ai un faible pour les sucreries.*
- An expression dating back to 14th century England, when **to have a tooth for** (sth) meant **to have a taste for** (sth). For the French, **un faible pour** means a weakness, **a soft spot for**...

He lies through his teeth.   *Il ment effrontément/Il ment comme il respire.*
- A medieval idiom implying a deceiving smile as a means to make the lie more credible. For some people, lying is as easy, or natural, as breathing.

Exercise: Research and provide equivalent idioms in French.

1. To go over (sth) with a fine-tooth comb _____

2. The tooth fairy (an animal for the French) _____

3. As bad as pulling teeth _____

4. It sets my teeth on edge _____

24. Throat:

I have a frog in my throat.   *J'ai un chat dans la gorge.*
– A croaky sound as one produced by a frog. For the French, why a cat? Apparently, the expression came from a 12th century play on words: **maton**, meaning milk curd, and **matou**, meaning tomcat. The word **chat** came later to replace **matou**.

He jumped down my throat.   *Il m'a sauté à la gorge.*

He shoves his ideas   *Il veut me faire avaler ses idées/*
down my throat.   *faire avaler des couleuvres*
– Force-feeding implies reluctance.

They are at each other's throats.   *Ils se sautent à la gorge/Ils s'étripent/Ils sont à couteaux tirés/ Ils sont comme chien et chat.*

A cutthroat practice   *une pratique coupe-gorge/ férocement compétitive.*
– Dates back to early 19th century as an adjective.

Exercise: Research and provide equivalent idioms in French.

1. To clear your throat _____

2. To cut your own throat _____

3. To go for the throat _____

4. To have a lump in your throat _____

25. Thumbs:

To have a green thumb   *avoir la main verte*
– The green color appears to come from a stain on the fingers of

people who handled vegetables or earthen pottery with plants.

To twiddle your thumbs   *se tourner les pouces*
– From a 15th century literal meaning of turning one's thumbs absent-mindedly, this expression came to mean *"to do nothing constructive"*.

He gave me the thumbs up.   Il m'a donné le feu vert./Il m'a fait un signe d'encouragement.
– It seems to have originated in Ancient Rome as a gesture to decide on the fate of a defeated gladiator: It was either thumbs up (live) or thumbs down (die).

He is all thumbs.   *Il est empoté./maladroit de ses mains*
– A thumb needs opposing fingers for grabbing and handling. Otherwise the result is clumsiness. For the French, **empoté** comes from old celtic *"paut"* (patte), meaning left hand or paw, thus considered gauche in those days.

As a rule of thumb   *en règle générale*
– This expression comes from an 18th century English law stipulating that a man can beat his wife with a stick not thicker than the thumb! Luckily, this idiom has lost its original meaning.

Sticking out like a sore thumb   *évident comme le nez au milieu de la figure*
– Already in use in the 16th century, this image stands for something or someone conspicuously present and particularly out of place.

Exercise: Research and provide equivalent idioms in French.

1. To thumb/hitch a ride _____

2. To be under someone's thumb _____

3. To thumb through (a book) _____

26. Toes:

Keep on your toes.   *Restez sur vos gardes./*
Soyez vigilants.
- From the idea of lifting oneself up to view better or farther, the expression means to be vigilant, alert and energetic for a task.

Don't step on her toes.   *Ne lui marchez pas sur les pieds.*
- The toes are a particularly sensitive part of the body. This expression is used to emphasize the seriousness of meddling in someone else's business, responsibility or prerogative.

To tiptoe/walk on tip toes.   *Marcher sur la pointe des pieds/*
Avancer avec prudence/Marcher
sur des œufs
- Either literally of figuratively, the idea is to advance cautiously and silently.

You have to stay on your toes.   *Vous devez rester sur vos gardes/*
éveillé/vigilant

Exercise: Research and provide equivalent idioms in French.

1. From head to toe _____

2. This made my toes curl (metaphor) _____

3. To deep your toe in the water (metaphor) _____
_____

27. Tongue:

This politician should bite/hold his tongue...   *Ce politicien devrait tenir sa langue/se taire/la boucler*
- Dating back to the 16th century, this expression means to refrain from speaking, biting being a painful reminder. For the French, **la boucler** means to "*buckle up*" one's tongue/shut one's mouth.

To avoid a slip of the tongue.   *éviter un lapsus linguae.*
– An involuntary statement uttered before judicious thinking. The French expression has the same meaning, but it borrowed the existing Latin term.

This word is on the tip   *J'ai ce mot sur le bout de la*
of my tongue.   *langue.*
– "**On the tip**" projects the belief of a near success in memory.

(She spoke) tongue-in-cheek.   *à prendre avec un grain de sel/ pince-sans-rire.*
– A statement accompanied by pushing the cheek with the tongue on one side of the face, to signal to an audience that the words are not to be taken seriously. For the French, **pince-sans-rire** was originally the name of a game in which players would pinch their partners with sticky fingers, probably without laughing. Used here as an adverbial phrase.

Exercise: Research and provide equivalent idioms in French.

1. To be tongue-tied _____

2. The cat got your tongue? _____

3. He has a loose tongue._____

4. He has a sharp tongue. _____

5. To speak with a forked tongue _____

6. My mother's tongue _____

IV. English idioms relating to areas of life and the environment

The physical environment has provided an abundance of images and metaphors to express in a more vivid, and at times visceral way, the various activities of our lives. Concrete objects and processes make abstractions come alive.

1. Business

Back to the drawing board *Retour à la case départ*
- Inspired by an architect or draftsman's blueprint, this idiom has been applied generally since WWII to many total changes of plans. In French, with a similar construction, it looks like a play in the well-known game of Monopoly...

The ball's in your court. *La balle est dans votre camp./A vous de jouer.*
- From sports, e.g. tennis, and applied generally to negotiating.

To be in it for the long haul *y être pour le long terme*
- An early 19th century expression from travel and transportation of goods. Generalized today to long term situations.

To burn one's bridges *couper les ponts*
- Note the change of images from burning to simply cutting, separating.

To put (something) on the back burner *mettre (quelque chose) en veilleuse*
- A 1940s idiom from newly conceived cooking stoves. Today it applies to projects of low priority, requiring no immediate attention. For the French, **une veilleuse** is originally a lamp of low intensity, allowing sleep. It is also the pilot light for an appliance (e.g., a stove or hot water heater).

The bottom line is that...   Le résultat/L'essentiel est que.../En définitive...
– A generalization from accounting, to mean the end result of a project or situation.

To be in the red   être à découvert (banque)/être en déficit
– This idiom apparently originated in early 20th century accounting, when a negative entry in a statement was written down in red ink. *A découvert* means without protection. It used to describe a situation when an army faced fire from the enemy in the open, without cover. It is applied now to a debt without endorsement or warranty.

Red tape   la paperasse/paperasserie/formalités administratives/la bureaucratie
– Out of several theories regarding its origin, it is generally believed that the idiom "**red tape**" came from the red ribbon that tied some official, very important documents from a king (perhaps Charles V of Spain). Today, it is a synonym of official bureaucracy.

Big deal!   La belle affaire!
– In Old English, **a deal** meant an amount. In mid-20th century, **big deal!** acquired its ironic meaning for an unimportant or insignificant situation.

Exercise: Research and provide equivalent idioms in French.

1. Let's call it a day _____

2. This restaurant is out of business _____

3. She means business! _____ _____

4. Let's get back to business _____

5. This is monkey business! _____

2. Clothing

At the drop of a hat — *sans hésiter/sans hésitation/à tout moment*

— Whether Irish or American West in origin, the drop of a hat signaled the start of a race or a fight.

To be in your shoes — *être à ta place /dans tes pompes*

— The French **pompes** refers to an earlier type of shoe. Today it is slang for *chaussures*.

To be out of it — *être à côté de ses pompes*

— In this expression from the mid-19th century, **pompes** has become slang. It means out of focus, the shoes in one direction, the head in another!

To handle (sb) with kid gloves — *prendre (qqn) avec des gants/ne pas le brusquer*

— Originated in the 18th century, this English expression was based on the finest leather, called kid leather. Gloves made of such leather were best suited for delicate tasks.

I'll eat my hat. — *Je me fais moine/Je me fais pendre*

— Until not long ago, hats were worn habitually. And felt was a material that required certain chemicals, which turned out to cause illness (*the hatter's shake*). Eating one's hat seemed to be more serious than having an unpleasant taste; it was an extreme show of confidence in a challenge! For the French, *se faire pendre* (to have oneself hanged) is not a pleasant experience.

My hat off to you! — *Chapeau!/Je vous tire mon chapeau.*

— In many situations, uncovering one's head, e.g., removing a helmet after a medieval tournament to reveal one's identity, was also a show of respect and at times submission. Today, it often shows admiration.

To talk through one's hat — *parler à tort et à travers/raconter n'importe quoi*

– The origin of this expression is uncertain, but it seems to echo another one: *"to talk from the top of one's head."* Both expressions probably point to the empty space above the head, and thus the purely speculative aspect of the talk. For the French, **a tort et à travers** means without rhyme or reason.

If the shoe fits, wear it.   *Qui se sent morveux se mouche.*
– From the English 17th century expression: *"If the cap fits, wear it."* In other words, your criticism applies to yourself! The French suggests that when someone's own nose is full, it is up to him to blow it, instead of being concerned about other noses! **La morve** means snot.

Exercise: Research and provide equivalent idioms in French.

To lose one's shirt _____

To wear the pants _____

To tighten one's belt _____

To roll up one's sleeves _____

3. Colors

To feel blue   *avoir le cafard*
– **Blue** is a synonym of sad, depressed. Its use with that meaning goes back to Chaucer. There seems to be only speculation as to its origin. For the French, the word **cafard** has a strange history. From the Arabic **kafir**, meaning non-believer, then hypocrite, to the crawling insect, cockroach, and finally with the poet Baudelaire who used **cafard** as a metaphor for the **spleen**.

Green with envy   *vert de jalousie*
– Seems to come from Shakespeare's *Othello*, where jealousy is evoked as a *"green-eyed monster."*

Out of the blue   *inopinément/de façon inattendue*

– As in the idiom *"out of the clear blue sky,"* the color blue is used here as a noun and refers to the sky itself. A sudden and unexpected act or statement can thus bring to mind the image of lightning. For the French, the etymology of **inopiné** is without *"opinion,"* without any apparent reason.

To raise a red flag   *donner le signal d'alarme/signaler une faute*

– A red flag was raised in the 16th century to signal preparation for battle. It was later used to signal danger. Today, the expression has generalized into alarms of all sorts (e.g., traffic), and even to sports for calling foul.

To run a red light   *brûler/griller un feu rouge*

– From *"running through"* a light to the idea of *"burning it"* as the French here says, suggests a more serious mistake in French!

To scream blue (bloody) murder   *crier au meurtre*

– The French expression appears to come from the French **morbleu**, a euphemism for the blasphemous oath « **mort Dieu** » (similar to « **sacré bleu** »).

A brown-noser   *un lèche-bottes/lèche-cul (vulgar)*

– An obsequious person will go to no end, except metaphorically to a most specific end (pun intended!) to seek favors. See also *"to brown-nose"* in a previous section.

Exercise: Research and provide equivalent idioms in French.

1. To brown-nose _____

2. To give/get the green light _____

3. A golden opportunity _____

4. To show one's true colors _____

5. Caught red-handed _____

6. Once in a blue moon _____

7. To be tickled pink _____

4. Drinking and beverages

To drink someone   *faire rouler (qqn) sous la table*
under the table
- This idiom is found in 17th century English literature.

Binge drinking   *une beuverie/une soûlerie*
- This idiom appears to be of Belgian origin, from the name of a Walloon city, **Binche**, which in English became **binge**. A social, excessive mode of drinking. *Binge* can also be used for excessive eating. The French expression comes from *se saouler*, meaning to get drunk. Alternate expression: ***Se péter la ruche***, apparently coined by pop singer Pierre Péret; **la ruche** is slang for *le nez*.

A social drinker   *un buveur mondain*
- Someone who consumes alcohol on special occasions and usually in moderation. It's the opposite of a binge-driker.

Bottoms up!   *Cul-sec!*
- It is said that this idiom originated in a 16th century method of recruiting sailors: a shilling was dropped into the bottom of a mug of beer for the sailor to drink. Once the coin was reached, the sailor had, consciously or not, been enlisted! Today it has become a simple challenge. In the French expression, the word **cul** is not vulgar when referring to objects like a bottle, a cul-de-sac, etc.

Eat, drink and be merry.   *Bien faire et laissez dire.*
- A Biblical (in Ecclesiastes) expression stressing the brevity of life and the need to enjoy it. It means to ignore criticism, as long as your enjoyment is ethically good.

To be on the wagon   *être au régime sec/s'arrêter de picoler*
- This appears to be a short form of "*on the water-wagon*" (early

20th century). Also, prisoners, when transported on a wagon, were allowed to drink only water. In the French expression, ***picoler*** means to drink excessively. This idiom comes from an Italian wine, the ***piccolo,*** imported in the 19th century and later bottled near Paris. As the cost was charged by the length of time spent in the pubs rather than by the glass or bottle, people were led to drink fast and much. A bit like the happy hour of today!

He is off the wagon. *Il a replongé./Il s'est remis à picoler.*
- The most plausible version is the situation of prisoners taken to the gallows on a wagon after taking the last drink of their life.

To wet your whistle *se rincer le gosier/la dalle/ s'humecter les lèvres*
- An expression dating back to the 14th century (Chaucer's Canterbury Tales), whereby the whistle is a dry mouth in need of dampness. In the French expression, ***une dalle*** is a stone or concrete slab, a metaphor for the esophagus.

(A marriage) on the rocks *un mariage qui bat de l'aile*
- The English evokes a ship that ended up on the rocks during a storm. The French speaks perhaps of a wounded bird flapping its wings in vain.

Down the hatch! *dans le gosier/Cul-sec!/Derrière la cravate!*
- The English seems to originate from sea cargo, where freight disappeared into the hold, *down the hatch*. The French term ***cul-sec*** means till the bottom is dry.

To nurse a hangover *cuver sa cuite/faire passer sa gueule de bois*
- Like something left over (hung over) from an earlier time, excessive drinking has its temporary consequences. The French ***cuver*** means to place wine in a ***cuve*** (a cask), to complete fermentation. ***Une cuite*** refers to what has been cooked. ***cuver sa cuite*** means to complete the process resulting from over-drinking, "cooking, simmering." ***La gueule de bois*** is the dry and pasty sensation in the mouth after drinking alcohol excessively (***gueule*** is slang for mouth).

This is not my cup of tea.   Ce n'est pas mon truc.
– **Mon truc** means my thing, my way.

The happy hour   la bonne heure de l'apéritif/l'apéro
– The phrase may have originated in 1913, when in the U.S. Navy a
  "*Happy Hour Social*" was organized by navy wives on board of the
  USS Arkansas.

It's no use crying   Ce qui est fait est fait./Ça ne sert à
over spilled milk.   rien de pleurer sur les pots cassés.

This explanation   Cette explication ne tient pas
does not hold water.   debout.
– **Tenir debout** requires a solid base, or else it collapses.

Exercise: Research and provide equivalent idioms in French.

1. To binge drink _____

2. To sober up _____

3. Cheers!/Here's to you _____

4. To hold one's liquor _____

5. To drown one's sorrows _____

6. (A drink) on the rocks _____

7. Another round, please _____

8. To tread water _____

9. He can't hold his liquor _____

5. Food

She is the apple of my eye.   Je tiens à elle comme à la prunelle
                                   de mes yeux.

– This idiom is used in the Bible (Moses). In antiquity, it appears that the pupil was associated with an apple because of its shape. The idiom seems to have also been used throughout the Middle Ages, as well as by Shakespeare. In the French expression, **la prunelle** is a fruit (sloe). By analogy it is a synonym of the pupil of an eye.

A banana republic *une république bananière*
– Used first in early 20th century by American short story writer O. Henry to describe unstable Latin American countries relying on a single economic resource, banana export.

To go bananas/go nuts *devenir dingue/péter les plombs*
– There are many theories behind this English idiom, none totally credible! Perhaps it describes the excitement of an ape reaching for bananas… The French **dingue** means *crazy*, and it's an adjective derived from the verb **dinguer,** meaning to ramble, to rant. **Les plombs** are the electric fuses in a home (as in blowing a fuse).

To bring home the bacon *faire bouillir la marmite*
– Originated in Essex; couples used to compete for a side of bacon as a reward for not having quarreled for one year and one day. In French, **une marmite** is a cooking pot, a kettle.

To butter up (someone) *lui passer de la pommade*
– This idiom may have originated in India, where butter balls were thrown at the statues of gods in exchange for favors. In this French expression, **la pommade** is also quite explicit, used in the context of spreading or massaging an oinment on the body.

To chew the fat *discuter le bout de gras avec (qqn)*
– This idiom originated in the 19th century, and it meant cutting thin slices from a smoked ham and chewing on them while chatting with visitors. Earlier in England, the idiom meant to complain or gripe. Today the term **to chew** someone's "*rear end*" still means to complain.

The cream of the crop *la crème de la crème/le dessus du panier*
– This English expression was probably borrowed from the French **la crème de la crème.** The cream, the top and best part of the milk, is

used metaphorically in many situations to express superiority. An alternate idiom to **la crème de...** is another metaphor, **la fleur de...** (e.g., *la fleur de la jeunesse américaine*).

Food for thought   *de quoi réfléchir*
- Food associated with thinking brings to mind the process of digestion, whose duration allows time to ponder. The expression dates back to at least the 18th century. The verb **ruminate**, when used to mean thinking is another example.

To be in a jam   *être dans le pétrin*

- From a preserve where fruit are packed together, to the verb **jammed up,** and **traffic jam,** these expressions depict uncomfortable situations for people used to ample space. For the French expression, already in the 18th century **le pétrin** was a large box where the baker's dough was mixed and allowed to rise. Someone falling in the pétrin would have had a hard time to come out on his own.

In a nutshell   *en résumé/bref*
- As old as antiquity, this idiom is used frequently. (e.g., in Shakespeare's works), and the meaning is self explanatory.

To spill the beans   *vendre la mèche*
- As the old story goes, in Ancient Greece membership in an association was voted using black and white beans cast into a jar (an earlier version of *black-balling*). At times, the jar was tipped over and the result of the vote was prematurely revealed. The French original expression was **éventer la mèche** (*éventer* meant to uncover, open into the "*wind,*" the open air). **La mèche** was a wick for candles or explosives. The meaning was to reveal what should have remained secret, and later **vendre** replaced **éventer**, meaning to sell out, betray.

That takes the cake!   *C'est le comble!/le pompon!/le bouquet!*
- The English expression goes back to Ancient Greece, where a cake was the reward of a competition. Over time, the idiom has reversed into an ironic statement: from positive praise to condemnation. For the French expression, **un pompon** is an added-on object. It could be translated as "*That tops it all.*" As for **C'est le bouquet!**, it has nothing

to do with flowers. The bouquet here refers to the end of a fireworks show, where the best is kept till the end; it tops it all indeed. As it happened with **pompon**, the expression has turned sarcastic, a very French tradition!

Life is not a bowl of cherries *La vie n'est pas une partie de plaisir.*
- With a possible 18th century origin, the American expression "**Life is just a bowl of cherries**" is the title of a 1930s song by Ethel Merman.

I am paid peanuts. *Je gagne des clopinettes.*
- **Une clopinette** (diminutive of **une clope**) is a tiny cigarette butt, i.e., of no real value.

She is a tough cookie. *C'est une dure à cuire.*
- The English expression may have originated in the 17th century to describe an intelligent woman. It's also used as **She is a smart cookie** (elle est vive/futée).

To take with a grain of salt *ne pas prendre (quelque chose) pour argent comptant*
- The Latin origin is of interest: **salis** means **salt** and **wit**. This might explain the idea of interpreting with a critical mind (as salt makes food more palatable). It was in the 17th century that this metaphorical expression entered the English language. For the French expression, **argent comptant** means real cash, hard cash.

Back to the salt mine! *Retour au bagne!/aux galères!*
- Salt has a long history: The word **salary** comes from the Latin **salarium.** Roman soldiers received a part of their pay in salt. Additionally, the salt mine refers to the notoriously hard Siberian mines, where dissidents were sent to dig. Today, another "*salt*" idiom frequently used is of course "*with a grain of salt*"! In the French expression, **Bagne** and **galères** are types of prisons, where hard labor was a form of punishment.

The proof is in the pudding *On juge l'arbre à ses fruits.*
- This idiom is attributed to Cervantes, a short version for "*The proof of the pudding is in the eating.*" "**The proof**" here means the test.

Exercise: Research and provide equivalent idioms in French.

1. The Big Apple _____

2. Get someone out of a jam _____

3. A traffic jam _____

4. Icing on the cake _____

5. They are like two peas in a pod _____

6. A couch potato _____

7. A hot potato _____

8. That's the way the cookie crumbles _____
_____

9. Honey catches more flies than vinegar _____
_____

10. Don't put all your eggs in one basket _____
_____

6. Furniture and household

To have a lot on one's plate   *avoir du pain sur la planche*
– Too much to handle, like a large food serving. A century ago, the French idiom meant to have plenty of resources, since bread was baked in a large loaf so that it would last a long time. Farmers made their own loaves and kept them on a board (*une planche*), hanging from the ceiling. In modern times, as everyone is buying small loaves of bread from bakeries, the expression now means "*to have many items to handle in a short time.*"

To roll out the red carpet for...   *dérouler le tapis rouge pour...*
– A red carpet was literally unrolled to welcome royalty or higher dignitaries. This custom is still practiced in England.

To see the writing on the wall   *se rendre à l'évidence/Voir ce qui se prépare*

- From an Old Testament story about mysterious hand writing predictions on a wall during the Jews' captivity in Babylon. It means to be able to see the evidence of warning signs.

A skeleton in the closet   *un squelette/un cadavre dans le placard/quelque chose à cacher*

- In early 19th century England, the expression was "*a skeleton in the cupboard,*" referring to some disease. In Gothic literature, this refers to skeletons and ghosts, as well as the era of body-snatchers. The idiom has risen in popularity, and the cupboard became a closet in America (vs. England's water-closets!).

A drop in the bucket   *une goutte d'eau dans l'océan/pas grand chose*

Kick the bucket   *casser sa pipe*

- Several theories coexist regarding the origin of this expression, including a bucket kicked from under a standing man with a noose around his neck, be it suicide or execution. Another explanation speaks about a beam, called a "**bucket**," from which a pig hangs, and is kicked before its slaughter. There is only speculation as to the origin of this French idiom. **La pipe** may be a symbol of a man's life, especially someone who always had it in his mouth.: There is also the case of an actor playing the role of a pirate, and the actor died on the stage, letting out his pipe, which broke upon hitting the floor!

Born with a silver spoon in one's mouth   *né dans la soie/dans du coton*

- In olden days, spoons were carved in wood. Only wealthy families ate with silver spoons (forks were invented in the 16th century). It was customary in these families to give a child a silver spoon at birth.

To call a spade a spade   *appeler un chat un chat*

- The expression can be traced back to Plutarch and Erasmus. Today it might be interpreted as an anti-political correctness principle. For the French, **un chat**, originally **une chatte** (fem., these words were synonyms of the female pubic mound.) Speaking this word in this context was thus bypassing some social convention that must have existed over several periods.

To go to pot — *tomber à l'eau (plan)/aller à la dérive (economy)/se laisser aller (person)*

– The expression is traced to the 16th century, referring to cooking a leftover piece of meat. Since then it has been used as a metaphor for declining or failing.

Out of the frying pan and into the fire — *de Charybde en Scylla/ de mal en pis*

– An idiom from Laurentius Abstemius, 15th century Italian fabulist: A fable that was later incorporated among Aesop's fables. For the French expression, **Charybde** and **Scylla** were depicted as two monsters in Greek mythology, the second worse than the other. Sailors could escape one, often to end up into the other. In reality, Charybde was a large whirlpool in the straight of Messina, while Scylla was a set of rocks. Homer's Odysseus had to confront these dangers.

Exercise: Research and provide equivalent idioms in French.

1. To treat someone like a doormat _____

2. To sweep (something) under the rug _____
_____

3. To put your house in order _____

4. To put your foot in the door _____

5. The deal is off the table _____

6. I am part of the furniture _____

7. You are completely off your rocker _____
_____

7. Gambling

Not by a long shot   *de beaucoup/de loin*
- This English expression refers to two 19th century idioms: In England "*by a long chalk*," in the U.S. "*by a long shot.*" **Chalk** refers to marks on the wall of a pub in dart games; **shot** refers to target shooting at a distance.

Without a ghost of a chance   *sans l'ombre d'une chance*

You bet your life!   *Et comment!/évidemment!*
- From a 1947 CBS Radio game show.

Lay your cards on the table.   *Jouez cartes sur table*
- Obviously from card playing, applied to other situations requiring transparency, cunning and planning.

Don't push your luck.   *Ne joue pas avec le feu/Ne pousse pas ta chance*

Put your money where   *Les actes valent plus que les*
your mouth is   *paroles.*
- The English expression is of uncertain origin. Some say it comes from Ireland, others say it's from the U.S. game of poker...

To call someone's bluff   *mettre (qqn) au pied du mur*
- **Bluff** is from the Dutch **bluffen**, meaning to brag, to boast. To call means here to force to prove one's claim. Several theories exist for the French idiom: 1) from fencing, by pushing your adversary's back against a wall; 2) to challenge someone who claims he can climb a wall to show it; 3) the idiom is reminiscent of the proverb: « ***C'est au pied du mur qu'on voit le maçon*** », which means "*so you say you can build a wall... Show it.*"

To follow suit   *emboîter le pas/faire de même*
- From card games, originating in the 17th century. The French idiom is of unknown origin: **emboîter** is possibly related to placing your footsteps in someone else's, as inside a box, **une boîte**.

He has a card up his sleeve.　　*Il a une carte/un atout/dans sa manche*

– A 16th century idiom, when sleeves served as pockets, signifying a definite, though dishonest, advantage in a card game.

The cards are stacked against me.　　*Je n'ai aucune chance/Les dés sont pipés contre moi.*

– The English saying implies that future events, like cards, are set, as a result of someone's actions or fate. The French expression **piper les dés** means to "*load*" dice, to make them fall the way you want to win. In this case, the expression is a synonym of cheating.

When the chips are down...　　*En fin de compte/Quand les jeux sont faits...*

– This refers to casino chips at roulette: When they are down on the table, no change is expected or allowed.

Exercise: Research and provide equivalent idioms in French.

1. A poker face _____

2. To have a ghost of a chance _____

3. To bet your bottom dollar _____

4. A house of cards _____

5. To play your cards right _____

6. Lost in the shuffle _____

8. Health

To be alive and kicking　　*être bel et bien vivant/en pleine forme*

– Kicking is a sign of vitality and spiritedness.

To be a bag of bones　　*n'avoir que la peau et les os*

To look the picture of health *respirer la santé*
- The English origin is unknown, but perhaps it's a personification of a condition. For the French, literally breathing (**respirer**) health is a positive sign.

To be in tip top shape *être en excellente condition/au mieux de sa forme*

To kick the bucket *casser sa pipe/tirer sa révérence*
- For the French, in the Middle Ages, a révérence was the way to beg leave, meaning ask for permission, of a socially higher-up person; **tirer** describes the pulling backward of the foot.

To be pushing up daisies *manger les pissenlits par la racine*
- Probably from the custom of planting or depositing flowers over graves. **Pissenlits** (dandelion) is a traditional salad in France whose roots are of course underneath.

To give a clean bill of health *trouver (qqn) en parfaite santé*
- Probably from a 17th century certificate testifying that a ship had no infectious disease on board before entering a port.

To be on one's last leg *être au bout de son rouleau*
- The French refers to the wooden rods around which parchment texts were rolled back in the 14th century. **Rouleau** signifies life span in this saying.

To have a new lease on life *avoir un regain de vitalité*
- The English saying originated in the early 18th century, meaning recovery from illness.

To be under the weather *être mal fichu/être patraque/ne pas être dans son assiette*
- The original English expression was "*to be under the weather* **bow**." The bow was the side of the boat battered by bad weather, and sick sailors were sent below deck for protection against the weather. For the French, **assiette** means here spatial axes, as those used in aviation for an airplane. **Patraque** seems to derive from an italian term, **patacca**, meaning worthless.

Exercise: Research and provide equivalent idioms in French.

1. A bitter pill to swallow _____

2. To bite the dust _____

3. To be hard of hearing _____

4. To pull through _____

9. Money

To bank on (something, somebody) for...   *compter sur... pour...*
- This English saying probably dates back to when trust was first placed in banks...

To make big bucks   *s'en mettre plein les poches/gagner du fric*
- The term **buck** relates to deer skin, when in the American frontier it was considered an exchange currency. The French word ***fric*** may have a couple of origins. It may originate fron the verb ***fricoter***, which means to plot, to scheme. It may also come from the Arabic ***frick***, meaning wheat. In fact, another French slang term for money is ***du blé*** (wheat), as the English "*Do you have some **dough**?*"

They are a dime a dozen.   *Il y en a/On en trouve/à la pelle.*
- In English, an early 19th century announcement came out that some foods were as inexpensive as "*a dime a dozen.*" Eventually the expression would describe things of little value and easily available. For the French, ***à la pelle*** means "*by the shovelful.*"

For a lousy buck   *pour un méchant dollar/pour un miserable centime*
- Both **lousy** and ***méchant*** are derogatory terms usually applied to actions rather than things. Here the dollar is metonymically affected by the action.

The pay is chicken feed.   *C'est un salaire dérisoire*
- Grains for chickens have to be small enough to be ingested and digested.

To work for peanuts	*bosser pour presque rien/pour des prunes*

– Peanuts were considered of little value for a long time, perhaps due to their size, availability, and price. Legend or history, the French idiom goes back to the second crusade at the end of the 12th century, which ended in a failure. The King is said to have asked: "*Are you telling me that you went to this crusade for plums? (**des prunes**).*" In the Middle-East, the crusaders had indeed tasted and brought back unknown plum trees to replant home! **Bosser** is a verb originally meaning **to bend over** some work, like a **bosse** (a hump). Today, it means to toil, to break one's back.

The other side of the coin	*le revers de la médaille*

– **Coins** and **médailles** can only be seen one side at a time.

To be broke	*être fauché/être à sec*

– **Broke** is the archaic form of **broken**, meaning bankrupt, ruined. *The complete French expression is « **être fauché comme les blés.** » **Faucher** means to cut, to reap. **Le blé** is a slang term for money.*

To pay in cold, hard cash	*payer en espèces (sonnantes et trébuchantes)/en argent liquide*

– Gold and silver being warm and soft to the touch, they also tended to wear out, so the metals were replaced by alloys that were colder and harder, and by paper money. For the French, **espèces** means species, denominations, i.e. in cash. **Sonnantes** is the particular sound of coins. **Trébuchantes** is derived from a special scale used to weigh gold and silver to determine their authenticity: **un trébuchet**.

To pay through the nose	*payer le prix fort/la peau des fesses*

– In the 9th century, Denmark invaded Ireland and imposed a tax "*on the nose,*" so one "*tax per nose,*" as a census method. Also, those who could not pay had their noses cut off! That was probably as painful as losing "*the skin of one's buttocks*" (*fesses*) in French, a strange form of scalping.

A penny for your thoughts	*A quoi penses-tu? Qu'est-ce qui te tracasse/Qu'est-ce qui te fait sourire?*

– A 16th century English expression found in Thomas More's *Four Last*

Things, and popularized the following century by John Heywood's book of proverbs.

To pinch pennies *faire des économies de bouts de chandelles*
- A fairly recent English idiom, first recorded in the 1940s. Pennies being of little value, pinching them is hardly worth it, just like saving pieces of candles, as stated by the French equivalent.

To be dirt poor *être dans la misère/dans la mouise/être fauché comme les blés*
- In the old days, the very poor lived in houses with compacted dirt floor, as they could not afford slate, stone or brick materials. For the French sayings, **la mouise** comes from the German **mues** (puree, mashed potatoes), probably a euphemism; **faucher** means *to cut*, as in cutting hay, corn.

Exercise: Research and provide equivalent idioms in French.

1. To bank on doing... _____

2. A blank check _____

3. To pick up the tab _____

4. It's worth its weight in gold. _____

5. To make a fast buck _____

10. Music

... and all that jazz. *et tout le bazar/et tout le bataclan*
- Of African origin, the word **jazz** referred initially to energy and even sexual stamina, but it lost this meaning over time. The expression was the title and refrain of a song in the musical <u>Chicago</u>, and today, it is a synonym of "*Et cetera.*" For the French sayings, **bazar** comes from a Persian word for a market, while **bataclan** appears to be an

onomatopoeia (ba-ta-clan) of an object falling in several stages. Both words refer to an unusual amalgam of things or disparate series of events.

To blow one's horn — *se péter les bretelles/se faire mousser*
- There is nothing like a trumpet to draw attention to the player. The English expression is already found in Matthew's gospel. In French, another way of attracting attention is to pull on one's suspenders (*les bretelles*) and make them snap (one of many meanings for *péter*), a sign of self-satisfaction as well. ***Se faire mousser*** alludes to stirring soap to produce an excessive volume of foam, a metaphor for seeking unjustified, empty fame.

To fine tune (a project) — *peaufiner/fignoler (un projet)*
- In the French expressions, ***peaufiner*** is related to ***peau*** (skin), and ***fin*** (fine, smooth), is close to the English verb ***refine***. ***Fignoler*** was already in Trévoux' Dictionary (18th century), meaning to make *finer*.

It's music to my ears! — *Douce musique à mes oreilles!/ Cela me met du baume au cœur.*
- The French ***du baume*** means balm, ointment in this case having a comforting effect, soothing the heart.

The boss calls the tune (or the shots). — *C'est le patron qui mène la danse.*
- The English apparently originates from a medieval proverb: "*He who pays the piper calls the tune.*" This is reminiscent of Molière's ***maître à danser***, the French idiom applying to all sorts of situations describing leadership. It may be slightly ironic in actual use.

It rings a bell. — *Cela me dit/me rappelle quelque chose.*
- The English expression may stem from the experiments of Russian scientist Ivan Pavlov, who used bells to trigger salivation in animals and assess the role of their memory.

This strikes a chord. — *Cela touche une corde sensible.*
- Obviously from the string instrument context, this English

expression is used metaphorically to mean causing an emotional response.

He plays second fiddle/   *C'est un sous-fifre.*
is a second banana.
- A musician is often called by the name of his/her instrument. **A second fiddle** is thus a musician occupying a secondary position in the orchestra, compared to the first violin. **Top banana** comes from vaudeville comedy, and it originated when a comic was given a banana after a particularly funny punch line; **second banana** was coined afterward for the lesser role. In the French example, **un fifre** is a wooden flute. **Un sous-fifre** stands for a musician or any other professional who plays a subordinate role.

It sounds like a broken record.   *C'est la même vieille rengaine./On dirait un disque rayé.*
- In French, **une rengaine** is a tune or song heard too many times, *"the same old tune."* **Rengaine** is a 17th century synonym of **refus**. A disk is said to be **rayé** when it has scratches.

He blew the whistle   *Il a vendu la mèche sur sa société*
on his company
- The idiom originated in 19th century England, when policemen were ordered to blow their whistles to alert the public of the presence of pickpockets and shoplifters. The situation was later reversed, and citizens began alerting the police.

To drum up support for...   *battre le rappel en faveur de...*
- The English comes from the old military expression *"to drum up recruits,"* using fife and drum.

Exercise: Research and provide equivalent idioms in French.

1. He no longer sings the same tune _____

2. To face the music _____

3. I know the score _____

4. To preach to the choir _____

5. He changed his tune _____

6. I'll have to play it by ear _____

11. Nature

A breath of fresh air   *une bouffée d'air frais/d'oxygène*
– In both languages, this refers to a new, refreshing wave of air replacing vitiated air, and it can be metaphorically applied to persons and situations.

To be in deep/in hot water   *être dans de beaux draps*
– **Deep water** can be dangerous for the unprepared or incompetent swimmer. To be **in hot water** suggests some wrong has been committed, and consequences are approaching. The original 17th century French idiom was « dans de beaux draps **blancs** », *draps* meaning sheets, and the white color being a sign of penance; *beaux* was added no doubt to infuse irony. **Drap** was also **fabric** for clothes and shrouds.

To beat around the bush   *tourner autour du pot*
– The idiom comes from the hunting practice of flushing birds from the underbrush, before "*cutting to the chase,*" i.e. finally aiming at the game. Beating the bush can also mean wasting time, especially around, instead of <u>at</u> the bush. The French expression originates in the 15th century, describing the cooking of a pot in a fireplace as a temptation and with hesitation (around, not in the pot) to steal unnoticed a succulent piece of meat. It is applied now to any situation in which a frank and direct action is needed.

To build castle in the air   *bâtir des châteaux en Espagne*
– Both languages speak of castles indeed, but why would the French have difficulty building castles specifically in Spain? The answer may be related to how the Moors made it impossible for French knights waging war in Spain to settle and build their castles on Spanish soil.

To come under fire   *essuyer le feu (ennemi)/*
                            être mis sur la selette

– In the first French expression, ***essuyer*** means to endure, to suffer through a situation. The second expression originates in the 13th century, when ***la selette*** was a short seat designed to place the accused at a low level for intimidation. Today the idiom means to be subjected to criticism.

Rain or shine, (we are going...)   *Qu'il pleuve ou qu'il vente...*

Can't see the forest for the trees.   *C'est l'arbre qui cache la forêt.*
– An old saying dating back to the Middle Ages, the archaic phrasing ***for the trees*** meaning *because of the trees.* The trees mean the details of a situation, as opposed to *"the big picture."*

She is down-to-earth.   *Elle a les pieds sur terre/Elle est terre-à-terre*
– "Down-to-earth" means pragmatic and realistic. In the French sayings, having ***les pieds sur terre*** is positive, while being ***terre-à-terre*** often indicates a low intellectual discernment.

We shall weather that storm.   *On affrontera la tempête.*
– In both languages, the English originating in the 17th century, the meaning is ***to go through*** a storm or an adverse situation and be successful in the end.

Exercise: Research and provide equivalent idioms in French.

1. A drop in the bucket _____

2. To gain/to lose ground _____

3. Don't make waves. _____

4. To go with the flow _____

5. It's the tip of the iceberg. _____

6. In virgin territory _____

12. Numbers

To be on cloud nine   *être au septième ciel*
- The International Cloud Atlas listed some time ago the cumulonimbus as the highest cloud (cloud 9), reaching some 60,000 feet. Metaphorically, it means bliss. The French expression makes reference to ancient astronomy, where each planet of our solar system was given a numbered sphere. The seventh sphere, or seventh heaven, was the realm of the gods.

To be dressed up by the nines   *être tiré à quatre épingle*
- For the English expression, no clear evidence is found explaining the number nine, other than it was often a symbol of perfection during the Middle Ages. The 17th century French expression describes the absence of wrinkles in a fabric stretched tight by pins at the four corners.

You look like a million dollars   *Vous êtes superbe!/magnifique.*

Give me a (high) five   *Tope là!*
- The **high five** originated a few decades ago as a congratulatory "*hand shake*" used in sports, baseball in particular. It is used today in many other situations. **Toper** comes from the old French **tuper,** meaning to throw, hit, and was a gesture of acceptance of a deal or challenge; **là,** meaning here, there, refers to the hand. For ages and in various civilizations, the touch of hands has been a sign of mutual trust.

To take the fifth   *invoquer le cinquième amendement de la constitution/ refuser de répondre/éluder la question*
- This English expression means to invoke the fifth amendment of the American Constitution, whereby one does not have to answer a question. It can be applied humorously to any life situation.

Cheaper by the dozen   *Treize à la douzaine*
- This English saying may have originated from another expression, ***a baker's dozen,*** whereby an extra bread roll was added to an order of twelve. "*Cheaper by the dozen*" was also used as the title for a 1948 novel by Frank Bunker Gilbreth, Jr. and Ernestine Gilbreth Carey.

That makes two of us.	*Alors on est deux./A qui le dis-tu!*

- The French idiom could also be translated into English as *You are telling me!*

To give someone the third degree	*cuisiner quelqu'un/le passer à tabac*

- The English expression refers to the classification of interrogation levels by the police. The **third degree** was torture. Another way to say it was "*to grill*" someone. Today, the idiom describes pressure through an insistent series of questions. In the French saying, **cuisiner** refers to methods of heated interrogation that use refinement in the process. *Passer à tabac,* a 19th century expression, had nothing to do with tobacco. The word **tabac** in this idiom comes from a confusion with the 14th century Occitan verb **tabaster**, meaning *taper, frapper.* In modern French there's a verb, **tabasser,** which means to beat up.

To have a one-track mind	*n'avoir qu'une idée en tête/ne penser qu'à ça*

- This English saying probably comes from early railroads, which had only one set of tracks, allowing for trains to pass in only one direction at a time. Today, the French idiom often describes a sexual obsession, thinking of only that (*ça*).

A catch-22 situation	*une impasse/un cercle vicieux*

- This idiom originated with John Heller in his 1961 novel Catch-22, in which he describes a conflictual situation in the Air Force: A pilot could request to be excused from flying based on insanity. But if he did, he was considered of sane mind, a "*damned if you do, damned if you don't*" situation indeed! The number was originally 18, but was changed to 22 because it sounded better.

Exercise: Research and provide equivalent idioms in French.

1. To be on all four _____

2. I am the fifth wheel. _____

3. First come, first served. _____

4. Never in a million years! _____

5. To look out for number one _____

6. Choose the lesser of two evils _____

13. Religion

To act high and mighty　　　*se donner de grands airs/être arrogant*
- The English idiom is a 15th century expression honoring the people in power. Since then, it has acquired a derogatory connotation. We have become more democratic!

An act of God　　　*une catastrophe naturelle/un acte de Dieu*
- A 13th century English expression describing a situation attributed to God's will. Since the 19th century, the expression has been used chiefly by the legal profession to describe a situation out of human control and thus eliminating any human responsibility.

It's a blessing in disguise.　　　*C'est un bien pour un mal.*
- Apparently a 17th century English idiom. There is also the French proverb « *A quelque chose malheur est bon* », that strikes a positive note in an apparently bad situation.

It's the blind leading the blind.　　　*Les deux se valent/C'est un aveugle qui en conduit un autre.*
- From an ancient Hindu sacred text, and found later in Matthew's gospel, the English idiom is a metaphor generally used to describe incompetence coupled with ignorance.

To catch/to get hell　　　*se faire attraper/se faire engueuler*
- This English hyperbolic expression means "*to get reprimanded*." Similarly, "*all hell breaks loose*" (from the 16th century) describes a situation changing for the worse. In the second French expression, ***engueuler*** derives from ***gueule***, which is slang for ***bouche***. ***La gueule*** is properly applied to noisy and ferocious animals. ***Engueuler*** means to be yelled at/chewed up.

To raise hell	*tempêter/faire une scène*

– The origin of this English expression is uncertain. It is perhaps an allusion to the netherworld, a very noisy and chaotic place raised up to earth by anger.

To scare the hell out of someone	*ficher/foutre (vulgar)/la trouille à (qqn)*

– Perhaps **hell** is assimilated to "*crap*," as in the almost identical expression, and fear will indeed produce such an effect, literally. ***La trouille**,* in the second part of the French idiom, is precisely that same effect.

Get the hell out of here!	*Casse-toi!/fiche le camp!/fous-moi le camp!*
Damned if I do, damned if I don't.	*Quoi qu'on fasse, on a toujours tort/on ne peut pas gagner.*
Just for the hell of it	*Comme ça/juste pour le plaisir*

– It's unclear how the word **hell** ended up meaning "*for no specific purpose.*" Was it simply on a whim? Doing something for the hell of it has got to be ironic, for who would want to go to *hell*?

When hell freezes over	*à la Saint-Glinglin/quand les poules auront des dents*

– For the French expression, there is no such saint! The word comes from the German verb **klingen**, meaning to sound, to ring, and a verb from the Champagne region dialect: ***glinguer**.*

I have been to hell and back.	*J'en ai vu de toutes les couleurs /J'en ai bavé.*

– This English phrase is often used to express the mythical fate of the hero, who must survive an ordeal and often death. The French expression's origin is uncertain. It probably derived from another one: « *En voir des vertes et des pas mûres* » , meaning to have seen it all, evoking an unpleasant taste (like a green, unripe fruit). The expression « *de toutes les couleurs* » would seem to multiply implicitly unpleasant experiences. In the 19th century, **en baver** meant "*to drool with astonishment.*" It gradually came to mean to suffer.

To hold out the olive branch *offrir la branche d'olivier*
- In both languages, this is a symbol of peace that originated in Greek mythology and spread throughout the Mediterranean world.

To be in limbo *être dans l'incertitude/ comme l'oiseau sur la branche*
- The English idiom originated from an early Catholic concept of a place between heaven and hell where non-baptized souls were temporarily placed. The word **limbo** actually came from the Latin **limbus**, meaning edge. Today the expression is used to describe any stagnant situation. Depending on the context, it is to be stuck in an uncertain situation, out of one's control.

A land of milk and honey *un pays de cocagne*
- The English expression refers to an Old Testament episode, when God promised Moses to bring the people of Israel to a land of plenty. The French idiom refers to **cockayne**, an imaginary blissful land throughout Europe in the Middle Ages, the opposite of the harsh conditions of peasant populations trying to survive; in short, a land of plenty.

To move heaven and earth for... *remuer ciel et terre pour.../faire des pieds et des mains pour...*
- The second French expression is an 18th century idiom describing the use of feet, in addition to hands, in an effort to obtain something, including success.

To preach to the choir *prêcher à des convertis/enfoncer des portes ouvertes*
- *Enfoncer des portes ouvertes*: No need to break down doors that are already open. The same is true for the choir, that needs no convincing, since it is already "*open*" to the source!

The devil is in the details. *Le diable est dans le détail/Plus facile à dire qu'à faire.*
- In both languages, the saying is attributed to Gustave Flaubert, who is thought to have said originally: « **Le bon Dieu** est dans les détails », The Devil instead of God certainly makes the situation more ominous.

Exercise: Research and provide equivalent idioms in French.

1. Speak of the devil... _____

2. It's gospel truth _____

3. It's as hot as hell! _____

4. The almighty dollar _____

5. (Someone) as ugly as sin _____

6. Holier-than-thou _____

7. To play the devil's advocate _____

14. Sports

It's a whole new ball game   *C'est une autre paire de manches.*
- Already used in the 16th century, the French expression may have originated from the medieval custom of sewing garment sleeves only temporarily to make them interchangeable.

To get back in the game   *rentrer dans la danse/être de retour en selle*

To be on the ball   *être à la hauteur de la situation/ être attentif*
- The English idiom may have been a contraction of "*keep your eyes on the ball.*"

(It) beats me.   *Ça me dépasse.*
- The origin of the expressions is uncertain in both languages. The meaning in English is "*It baffles me,*" "*I am at a loss to answer.*" The French meaning is *It is above my head/It's beyond me.*

To play hard ball   *jouer dur/ne pas faire de cadeaux*
- Unlike softball, baseball uses a hard ball, making for a more aggressive and competitive game. The English idiom seems indeed to come from the game of baseball. In French, the player gives his all, does *no favor*, gives *no easy ride* to the opponent.

To throw in the towel   *jeter l'éponge/déclarer forfait*
- **To throw in the towel** comes from boxing, as a sign of accepting defeat. In French, **un forfait** is the act of giving up.

She calls the shots.   *C'est elle qui mène la danse.*
- This idiom has two possible origins in English: 1) Whoever is in charge of the target calls its position or signals when to shoot, or 2) In a game of pool, the player indicates in advance the shot he/she plans to make.

To get into the swing of things   *se mettre dans le bain*
- Golf may be the origin of this English expression. At any rate, the expression has to do with the rhythm, the pace and the ways of an activity. From an early 20th century idiom meaning "*to be implicated,*" the French idiom has evolved into a more positive context: *to be fully involved* in, and at ease with a project.

To go overboard on (sth)   *s'emballer pour (qqch)/exagérer*
- The English idiom refers to the railing of a boat or ship, over which one can fall if leaning too far. ***S'emballer,*** means *to bold*, like a horse out of control. At the human level, it is an image for uncontrolled enthusiasm.

To hit below the belt   *faire un coup bas*
- An illegal blow in boxing. Can be applied to any unfair or ugly attack.

To hit a snag   *tomber sur un os/Il y a un hic!*
- In the English idiom, the unlucky soldier "*fell on a branch*" (from **snagi**, meaning protruding branch, possibly of 16th century Scandinavian origin). It may have entered the English language in the 19th century as a figurative image for encountering an obstacle. The French idiom « *tomber sur un os* » originated in WWI, with soldiers' food rations. Some rations were mostly bone with a bit of meat around it! **Un hic** comes from Latin: "*Hic jacet lepus,*" meaning here lies the hare, an unexpected obstacle.

He is a big shot.   *un grand ponte/un gros bonnet/ une grosse légume*
- **Big shot** used to refer to a gun caliber, then to the bearer of such gun.

The idiom came from the prohibition era of gangsters (1920s). Was it that the bigger the gun, the more important one seemed to be?

You are off base. *Vous êtes dans l'erreur/vous vous trompez/vous n'y êtes pas.*
– The English idiom probably originates from the game of baseball, where for a player to wander a distance from a base is a mistake. Similarly, a base is used figuratively to mean solid, safe ground in thinking.

The project is on target. *Le projet se déroule comme prévu.*

There are plenty of fish in the sea. *Un(e) de perdu(e), dix de retrouvé(e)s*
– Apparently a 16th century English idiom used as a consolation for lost opportunity or relationship, especially a romantic relationship.

To settle the score with (sb) *régler son compte à/avec. (qqn)...*
– A term of ancient accounting, whereby debts were marked on a **tally** (a stick) in which **scores** (marks) were notched. Apparently, the old system survived in England till the early 19th century. Today, the expression has taken the negative connotation of achieving revenge.

I'll take a rain check. *On remet ça à une autre fois./à une prochaine fois.*
– The custom to issue a replacement ticket for a cancellation due to unforeseen rain seems to have originated in late 19th century in the United States, whether for a game or an open-air vending booth... As a metaphor, the idiom refers to the setting up of a new opportunity.

To set the bar too low/high *placer la barre trop bas/trop haut*
– Late 19th or early 20th century; the English expression comes from sports competitions in jumping and racing. Metaphorically, it refers to the setting of standards.

Exercise: Research and provide equivalent idioms in French.

1. The ball is in your court _____

2. At this stage of the game _____

3. The front runner _____

4. No sweat! _____

5. To get the ball rolling _____

6. To keep the ball rolling _____

15. Time

On the cusp of	*sur le seuil de/à l'aube de*
Better late than never.	*Mieux vaut tard que jamais.*
At the eleventh hour	*à la dernière minute/au dernier moment*

– The English expression occurs in Matthew's gospel (XX). The frequent use came later, describing the last hour of a working day (from 6 a.m. to 6 p.m.), so the eleventh hour was from 5 to 6 p.m.. Today, it means *"at the very last moment."*

In the long run	*à la longue*
In my own sweet time	*quand bon me semble/à mon rythme*

– Unclear origin. The word **sweet** indicates lack of concern for the time of others.

It's just around the corner.	*C'est pour demain/C'est pour bientôt.*

– From the idea of space to time, as in *"The end of the year is just around the corner."*

This is the moment of truth.	*C'est l'heure/le moment/de vérité*

– An expression that possibly comes from a Spanish bull fight: The moment of truth is the instant when the matador prepares to plant his sword in the bull's neck. The truth may be about who is ultimately the victor.

Never in a million years.	*jamais de la vie/jamais, au grand jamais!*

I had the time of my life!	*Je me suis amusé comme un fou!/ Je me suis éclaté comme jamais.*

– This English expression is of unknown origin. *Time* in this context means experience, implying that it was very enjoyable. A synonymous idiom is *"to have a ball."*

Time is ripe.	*C'est le moment où jamais./Le moment est venu de…*

– The English expression was used, perhaps for the first time, by Shakespeare. Like a fruit ready to pick, the appropriate moment for action has arrived.

He lives on borrowed time.	*Il n'en a plus pour longtemps.*

– Borrowed from Death, like having *"a new lease on life,"* but the expectation of survival is short. This English expression originated in late 19th century.

To lose track of time	*perdre la notion du temps/ne pas voir passer le temps*

In the nick of time	*juste à temps/"in extremis"*

– A **nick** was originally (17th century) a notched stick marking a precise place. It was then applied to time, and particularly a precise instant, that often was the last one.

To play for time	*chercher à gagner du temps/ atermoyer*

– **To stall, to waste time** as a strategy. Why play? Perhaps to get more time to plan ahead. The strategy is like a game… The French **Atermoyer** also means to stall.

Let's call it a day.	*Ça suffira pour aujourd'hui./ Restons-en là.*

– This English expression originated in the early 20th century, when a worker ended his day's work before closing time. A day was a day's work. The original expression was *"call it a half-day."*

To serve time — *être en prison/purger une peine de prison*

- This English idiom is of uncertain origin. While to serve means to perform one's duty, *to serve time* means to go to prison as reparation for a crime. In the French idiom, the basic meaning of **purger**, from the Latin **purgare**, means to purify, to clean. **Purger une peine** means to clean, erase one's crime in any manner, including by a term in prison.

At the crack of dawn — *au point du jour/à l'aube/aux aurores*

- **Crack** is apparently an old English term meaning a sudden sound. The original meaning was applied to a sudden sight, the exact instant when the sun breaks on the horizon. The original phrase was *"the crack of day."*

She won big time! — *Elle a gagné de façon spectaculaire./haut la main.*

- The origin of the English expression is uncertain, although the idiom *"**big time**"* is traced to the early 20th century, meaning *"in a spectacular way."*

Long time no see. — *Ça faisait longtemps, hein!/Ça faisait un bail!/Ça faisait une éternité!*

- An American expression that appears to imitate pidgin English, or Native American talk in Western movies! In French **un bail** is a lease, i.e. a long-term contract. Certain leases, in farm lands, can be as long as 99 years.

You have made my day. — *Vous m'avez remonté le moral./Vous m'avez mis du baume au cœur.*

- The origin of this English expression is uncertain. In both languages, one's action or words brightened someone else's whole day.

Go ahead, make my day! — *Vas-y, fais-moi plaisir!*

– The English expression comes from the film <u>Sudden Impact</u>, where *Dirty Harry*, a character played by Clint Eastwood, challenges a robber to use his gun, meaning it would be a pleasure to "*dispatch*" him.

The shelf-life (of a product)   *la durée de vie/de validité (d'un produit)*
– In both languages, the expression refer to the duration of a product before its expiration date.

Exercise: Research and provide equivalent idioms in French.

1. A race against the clock _____

2. I knew it all along _____

3. Time after time _____

4. To have time on your hands _____

5. It's about time! _____

6. To stand the test of time _____

7. To best the clock _____

16. Travel

To be a backseat driver   *jouer/faire la mouche du coche*
– An early 20th century English expression born from the beginning of the automobile. It describes someone always criticizing and directing the actual driver. It may apply to situations unrelated to driving. The second French expression is from La Fontaine's fable « Le coche et la mouche », in which a fly claims falsely to direct the operation of a stagecoach.

The designated driver   *le conducteur désigné/le Sam*
– The "*designated driver*" English idiom actually came from a program

devised in Scandinavia and spread gradually to other lands, including Canada and the U.S.: A group designates one member as the driver, and that person is to remain sober until everyone including himself is safely back home.

To drive a hard bargain   *être dur en affaires/négocier ferme*
- This expression dates back to medieval England regarding cattle driving. Today, it refers to hard negotiating and bargaining.

You drive me up the wall!   *Tu me rends fou/Tu me tapes sur les nerfs/me fais grimper aux rideaux.*
- The origin of this English expression is uncertain. It conjures up an image of someone so exasperated, that he/she tries to escape by extreme means, such as climbing a wall.

To be the fifth wheel   *être la cinquième roue du carrosse*
- This English idiom originated in the 17th century, when it was customary to carry around a spare wheel, even if it was needed infrequently. As a metaphor, it applies to a person whose presence and action is considered unnecessary or unimportant. The French equivalent expression uses the word **carrosse**, which was an ancient vehicle, and thus confirms the 17th century origin.

I'll hit the road   *Je me tire*
- The English expression originally applied to horses stumping the pavement with their hooves. Applied to humans, it simply means to depart. It may have a negative connotation if used to tell someone to leave. The origin of the French idiom is uncertain; it refers perhaps to the idea of **pulling oneself** away from a place.

My way or the highway.   *C'est ça ou rien/C'est comme ça et pas autrement.*
- The English expression dates back to the 1970's, synonymous to "*Take it or leave it...*"

We are in the same boat.   *Nous sommes logés à la même enseigne./Nous sommes tous dans la même galère.*
- The meaning underlying the English idiom was already in use in

Ancient Greece. It gradually came to be applied to any precarious or perilous situation or condition. The French equivalent is a 16th century idiom, referring to the conditions and amenities found in an inn that one has chosen. All the guests shared the same comfort or lack of it! This applies now to all sorts of situations.

To miss the boat *rater/louper le coche/laisser passer une occasion*
- In the French expressions, **un coche** was not only a stagecoach, but also a fairly large riverboat, one that could not be missed and which came at regular intervals. **Rater** and **louper** are synonyms of **manquer**.

To rock the boat *faire des vagues/faire des histoires*
- The English expression is attributed to an American statesman, William Jennings Bryan, who used it in 1914 to refer to actions that create problems.

Off the beaten track *hors des sentiers battus*
- The English expression dates back to the 17th century, meaning out of the ordinary situations. Often applied to tourism or new projects.

To put the pedal to the metal *appuyer sur le champignon*
- Dating back to the 1950s, when metal was visible in car floors, the English expression meant to accelerate. It was then applied metaphorically with the meaning of speeding up a process. Regarding the French idiom, in mid-twentieth century, the accelerator pedals were often in the shape of a mushroom.

To take (someone) for a ride *mener (qqn) en bateau*
- This English idiom may have originated in the 1920s, at a time when the expression meant literally to take someone away in a car with the hidden intention to kill. Today, the expression has a milder meaning while still keeping the element of deception.

To be/to jump on the wagon *être/se mettre/au régime sec*
- This English expression seems to have originated at a time when water carts in the 19th century spread water on dusty roads. Men who pledged to stop drinking alcohol said they got on the water-wagon. The idiom was then reduced to just *"the wagon."*

| A middle-of-the-road approach | *une solution modérée/ intermédiaire* |

– This English idiom dates back to the late 19th century, as a political expression used to describe policies that were moderate and safe enough to be acceptable to all parties.

| Time to get the show on the road | *Il est temps de passer à l'action.* |

– This is an early 20th century English expression, at a time when theater groups and circuses traveled from town to town.

| To sail through an exam | *réussir (à un examen)/haut la main* |

– This is an English analogy to the smooth gliding of a sailboat on the water, a 19th century expression. The French **haut la main** may have originated from horseback riding: Raising the reins to control the horse.

| Let's burn rubber | *Appuyons sur le champignon* |

– Metaphorically, this English expression means to depart rapidly, as a car scorching tires on the road by way of acceleration. **Le champignon** was the term used to describe the shape of early car accelerators.

| To hitch a ride/to hitchhike | *faire de l'auto-stop/faire du stop* |

– In the 16th century, the English expression **to hitch a hike** meant to attach with a hook. In the early 20th century, it acquired the metaphoric denotation we know today.

Exercise: Research and provide equivalent idioms in French.

1. A Sunday driver _____

2. To be back on track _____

3. To hit the road _____

4. A hit and run accident _____

5. He drives a hard bargain _____

6. A carpool _____

7. I lost my train of thought _____

8. He talks a mile-a-minute _____

V. Miscellaneous English idioms:

(alphabetically by keywords)

Section 1:

To be better/worse off   *être mieux loti/plus mal loti*
- The French ***loti*** means subdivided; here it means comparatively better or worse in a given situation.

To be in a bind   *être dans le pétrin/la panade/la mouise*
- Apparently the English expression comes from lumberjacks. When a saw got squeezed and trapped in a tree, it was said to be "***in a bind.***" A synonym would be ***a tight spot***. In French, starting in the 12th century, ***le pétrin*** is a kneading trough for making bread. Presumably it would be difficult to pull out of there after a fall. ***Panade*** was a poor people's soup made with old bread, probably quite soggy and tasteless. ***Mouise*** was a purée. Those who ate these cheap foods were in a precarious economic situation.

To pass the buck   *refiler la responsabilité/renvoyer la balle*
- The English idiom apparently originated from the game of poker, where a knife with a buckhorn handle pointed at the next dealer.

The buck stops here.   *J'en assume la responsabilité.*
- The English expression was somewhat of a motto for President Harry Truman, who exhibited it on his desk. It indicates full responsibility for an action involving others and for its outcome.

To break the ice   *briser la glace*
- An English expression taken from navigation in cold waters. It

acquired its metaphorical meaning in the 16th century regarding awkward situations.

It's a cinch!   *C'est du gâteau!/C'est facile.*
- The English idiom comes from the Spanish **cincha**, a girth to keep the horse saddle firmly in place. Metaphorically, it stresses simplicity and ease.

He is a chip off the old block.   *C'est le digne fils de son père*
- An English idiom dating back to the 17th century.

He is the spitting image   *C'est son père tout craché.*
of his father.
- Apparently also a 17th century English expression, that would seem confirmed by modern DNA technology.

To find fault with...   *trouver à redire à...*

To get one's act together   *se réorganiser/mettre de l'ordre dans...*
- Probably taken from the theater environment, the English means to metaphorically reorganize oneself or one's actions.

To get cold feet   *se dégonfler/se rétracter*
- Attributed to either Ben Johnson, from England, or Stephen Crane, from the U.S., this English idiom means to be incapacitated by fear. In the French case, for the origin of *se dégonfler* is unknown, although we can imagine it refers to losing air, like a balloon.

I get a kick out of...   *J'éprouve un sacré plaisir à...*
- The origin of the English expression is uncertain. It may be a reference to a sudden release of adrenaline due to an emotion.

To get up on the wrong side   *se lever du pied gauche*
of the bed
- In ancient Rome, the wrong side was the **left** side, the Latin word for left being **sinistra**. A bad omen was attached to the idea of left, *sinister*.

Exercise: Research and provide equivalent idioms in French.

1. To bear in mind _____

2. To bridge the gap _____

3. To have a change of heart _____

4. A dead end _____

5. An eye-opener _____

6. For the time being _____

7. At 8 o'clock-ish _____

8. It crossed my mind _____

Section 2:

    Give it a shot.   *Tentez le coup/Tente ta chance*
    – The English may be of military origin, meaning trying, or attempting to hit a target. If so, it dates back to the 16th century.

    To give someone   *engueuler quelqu'un/passer une*
    a piece of your mind   *engueulade à...*
    – The origin of this English expression is uncertain. It's a synonym of a reprimand, a strong scolding. The French **engueuler** means to shout at someone.

    A gut feeling   *une intuition/un vague sentiment*
    – The English expression dates back to the physiology of Biblical time, when the guts were believed to be the seat of emotions.

    He has no clue   *Il n'en a pas la moindre idée.*
    – Apparently in the Renaissance **clue** was spelled **clew**, meaning a ball of thread, and a reference to mythology's Ariadne's ball of thread that gave Theseus a sense of direction.

    I have had it up to here.   *J'en ai marre/J'en ai ras le bol.*

– The reference to *it* in this English idiom is unclear. The whole idiom indicates frustration and a loss of patience with something or someone unpleasant. A synonym of being *fed up*. Among a number of theories as to its origin, the French word *mar* (sic) apparently meant to *share* in 19th century burglary circles, when several robbers formed a team. *Ras le bol* is an expression that used to be vulgar, as *bol*, a forgotten slang word, referred to the anus! A modern expression uses the term we know: *plein le cul* (vulgar).

There you go! (for approval)　　*Voilà!/Très juste!*

Home, sweet home!　　*Comme on est bien chez soi!*
– The English expression is actually the title of an 18th century American poem and subsequent song. Now a saying of satisfaction upon returning home.

The ins and outs (of something)　*les tenants et les aboutissants*
– The English idiom apparently dates back to the late 19th century, meaning all the detailed knowledge of an art, job, situation, story, etc. The French expression is from the 16th century, used in real estate to mean all pieces of land and constructions adjacent to, and part of, a property. Today, it has the more general meaning of all the details of a situation.

To jump the gun　　*agir prématurément*
– An early 20th century English idiom describing a false start, when one contestant departs in a race before the gun signal.

To know/learn the ropes　　*Connaître/apprendre les ficelles*
– This English expression is from the late 19th century, first used metaphorically to describe thorough knowledge of a situation or task. It was a nautical term related to the handling of sails. From rope to string in French, strings (*ficelles*) were originally a visible, artificial part of a mechanism. The negative connotation subsided in favor of practical, efficient knowledge.

To let off steam　　*se défouler/relâcher la pression*
– The English is a metaphor based on a boiler letting steam out to reduce the pressure. The French *se défouler* comes from the medieval verb *fuler/fouler*, meaning to trample; the prefix *dé-*

signals a decrease in pressure. Today, **se défouler** often means "*to get (something) out of one's system.*"

To make ends meet *joindre les deux bouts*
– Among several theories, the more plausible and original source for the English expression may have been a term of accounting: making the totals of two columns coincide.

There is nothing to it! *Il n'y a rien de vrai là-dedans. /C'est facile à faire.*
– There are two possible meanings for the English phrase: denial or easy task, two different situations indeed.

No way José! *Pas question!/Jamais de la vie!*
– A 1960s English idiom that originated in New York's guide Village Voice. **José** seems to be there only to rhyme with **way.**

To rip (someone) off *arnaquer/escroquer (quelqu'un)*
– The English expression is an African-American slang term from the 1960s.

Run-of-the-mill *tout à fait ordinaire*
– Originated in early 20th century, this English phrase referred to products before sorting for quality. It was metaphorically generalized in the 1920s.

Exercise: Research and provide equivalent idioms in French.

1. Out of sight, out of mind _____

2. Off the beaten track _____

3. For the long haul _____

4. To have mixed feelings _____

5. To keep track of _____

6. To look for a needle in a haystack _____

Section 3:

Safe and sound   *sain et sauf/à bon port*
- A 14th century English expression, when **sound** meant **whole**. Used now especially at the end of a trip. ***A bon port*** is a term of nautical navigation dating back to the 14th century (was then ***à droit port***).

Made from scratch   *fait maison/fait à partir de zéro/ entièrement à la main*
- Apparently from an 18th century English expression; a line was drawn by *scratching* the ground to mark a starting point in a game or a race. It gradually meant *from nothing, from zero*. Depending on the situation, these French equivalents will vary.

On second thought   *toute reflexion faite*
- A 17th century English expression, meaning reconsideration of a decision.

To be sick and tired of...   *en avoir assez de.../en avoir marre de...*
- The English expression originated in the 18th century, with the same meaning it has today. ***Marre*** comes from the ancient word ***mar***, meaning *share*. The idiom means to have had one's share (of a problem).

It completely slipped my mind.   *Ça m'est complètement sorti de l'esprit/j'ai complètement oublié.*

to throw a fit/to blow one's top   *piquer une crise/péter les plombs*
- ***A fit*** is a sudden emotion and its physical reaction. *Blow your top* apparently dates back to the Industrial Revolution, with the advent of steam power. In the French idiom, ***piquer*** means to prick, to pierce, with the nuance of suddenness as in ***une crise*** (*a fit*). ***Péter les plombs***, meaning *to blow a fuse*, refers to the protective lead wire that formerly connected two poles and burned easily under an intense electrical surge.

To throw in the towel   *jeter l'éponge*
- Also listed in the Sports section. Whether a towel or a sponge, the English expression probably originated in boxing, as a signal to stop

the bout. It became a metaphor for giving up.

To tie the knot *convoler en justes noces/se passer la corde au cou*

- Whether Celtic or Roman in origin, in many cultures the **knot** has stood for strong bonds, or commitment, in matrimony, appearing symbolically in weddings. The French expression comes from the Latin ***cum volare***, and the term ***convoler*** means to fly with, and *noces* comes from the Latin ***noptiae***. It's exclusively used in the context of marriage. ***La corde au cou*** is a cynical expression describing marriage as a total submission or condemnation!

She won big time *Elle a gagné et de loin/haut la main.*

- A 19th century American English phrase meaning *in a big way, to a great extent*.

I owe you big time. *Je vous dois une fière chandelle.*

- The French expression is derived from an old Catholic tradition of lighting a candle in church to God (or a saint) as a sign of gratitude. It is now applied in many non-religious situations.

(Something) is up in the air. *incertain/en suspend/encore vague*

- This 18th century English idiom refers originally to particles suspended in the air, not yet settled on the ground, and it has come to symbolize a matter or project which is still uncertain.

Exercise: Research and provide equivalent idioms in French.

1. Shame on you! _____

2. To stand/hold your ground _____

3. To set the record straight _____

4. You can say that again! _____

RECAPITULATION OF PART ONE

MATCHING EXERCISES

To aid in memorization, the following set of exercises provides a review of the idioms presented earlier. You are asked to match English idioms with their equivalents in French by matching the numbers of one list to the letters of the other list.

A few French similes:

1. Il chante comme une casserole. ( )

2. On entre ici comme dans un moulin. ( )

3. Il est comme un coq en pâte. ( )

4. Il ment comme il respire. ( )

5. Cela a marché comme sur des roulettes. ( )

6. Il se porte comme un charme. ( )

7. Je m'en moque comme de l'an 40. ( )

8. On est comme l'oiseau sur la branche. ( )

9. Ils sont comme les deux doigts de la main. ( )

10. Ils sont comme cul et chemise. ( )

11. Cela se vend comme des petits-pains. ( )

12. S'amuser comme des petits fous. ( )

a. He lies through his teeth **b.** We don't know which way to turn **c.** They are buddy-buddy. **d.** can't carry a tune **e.** They have a ball. **f.** He is as fit as a fiddle **g.** They just waltz in and out of here. **h.** He lives the life of Riley. **i.** They are like butter and toast. **j.** I couldn't care less about it. **k.** It went like clock-work. **l.** It sells like hot cakes.

I. SECTION ON ANIMALS

1. English idioms using birds, dogs, cats, and fish:

Match English and French idioms:

1. The early bird gets the worm. ( )

2. A little bird told me. ( )

3. All this work for the birds. ( )

4. It rained cats and dogs. ( )

5. It's the tail wagging the dog. ( )

6. He is in the dog house. ( )

7. Let sleeping cats lie. ( )

8. Quit pussyfooting around. ( )

9. We have bigger fish to fry. ( )

10. He is a cold fish. ( )

11. There is something fishy. ( )

a. Premier arrivé, premier servi. **b.** Il n'est pas en odeur de sainteté. **c.** Ne tourne pas autour du pot. **d.** C'est mon petit doigt qui me l'a dit. **e.** C'est un pisse-froid. **f.** Il tombait des cordes. **g.** On a d'autres chats à fouetter. **h.** C'est le monde à l'envers. **i.** Tout ce travail pour des prunes. **j.** Ne revenons pas là-dessus. **k.** Il y a quelque chose de louche.

2. English Idioms using horses, cows and bulls, and pigs:

1. Hold your horses. ( )

2. Don't put the cart before the horse. ( )

3. like a bull in a china shop ( )

4. Till the cows come home ( )

5. Let's ride piggyback. ( )

6. to pig out ( )

a. Montons à califourchon. **b.** Ne mets pas la charrue avant les bœufs. **c.** s'en mettre plein la lampe **d.** comme un chien dans un jeu de quilles **e.** Minute, il n'y a pas le feu. **f.** Quand les poules auront des dents.

3. English idioms using monkeys, rats, wild animals, and insects:

1. I got the monkey off my back. ( )

2. This is monkey business. ( )

3. He went ape. ( )

4. It's a rat race. ( )

5. We smell a rat. ( )

6. A leopard can't change its spots. ( )

7. He has ants in his pants. ( )

8. He has butterflies in his stomach. ( )

9. Don't bug me. ( )

10. Bug off. ( )

11. This put a bug in my ear. ( )

12. Don't let the bed bugs bite. ( )

a. Il y a quelque chose de louche. **b.** Lâche-moi le coude. **c.** Il a le trac. **d.** C'est la foire d'empoigne. **e.** On sent là une affaire louche. **f.** Je suis soulagé d'un poids. **g.** avoir la bougeotte **h.** Dégage/Du vent **i.** Chassez le naturel, il revient au galop. **j.** Fais de beaux rêves **k.** Ça m'a mis la puce à l'oreille. **l.** Il a pété les plombs.

4. English idioms using other animals:

1. She is an eager beaver. ( )

2. He has bats in the belfray. ( )

3. It's a kangaroo court. ( )

4. He is the black sheep of the family. ( )

5. It's the elephant in the room. ( )

6. He came bright-eyed and bushy-tailed. ( )

7. It's the straw that broke the camel's back. ( )

a. C'est la brebis galeuse de la famille. **b.** C'est la goutte d'eau qui a fait déborder le vase. **c.** C'est une bosseuse. **d.** Il arrivait tout pimpant. **e.** Voilà un tribunal fantoche. **f.** Il a des araignées au plafond. **g.** Voilà le gros tabou.

II. SECTION ON BODY PARTS

1. English idioms using arm, back, belly, bones, and brain:

1. Twist my arm. ( )

2. It was a shot in the arm. ( )

3. It costs an arm and a leg. ( )

4. Get off my back. ( )

5. You scratch my back and I'll scratch yours. ( )

6. I break my back for you. ( )

7. It went belly-up. ( )

8. He made no bones about it. ( )

9. I have a bone to pick with them. ( )

10. I wish to pick your brain. ( )

11. He is a scatter-brain. ( )

a. Fiche-moi la paix. **b.** Quel écervelé! **c.** C'est bien pour te faire plaisir. **d.** J'ai maille à partir avec eux. **e.** Je me coupe en quatre pour toi. **f.** Il a coulé. **g.** Ça m'a donné un coup de fouet. **h.** Il a dit les choses comme elles sont. **i.** Un service en vaut un autre. **j.** Puis-je faire appel à tes lumières? **k.** Ça coûte les yeux de la tête.

2. English idioms using chin, ears, and eyes:

1. Keep your chin up. ( )

2. It's music to my ears. ( )

3. He is wet behind the ears. ( )

4. Play it by ear. ( )

5. We see eye to eye. ( )

6. It was an eye-opener. ( )

7. (not awake) I can't focus. ( )

8. In the blink of an eye ( )

a. Il est né de la dernière pluie. **b.** en un clin d'œil **c.** Ça m'a ouvert les yeux. **d.** Garde la tête haute./Tiens bon **e.** Je n'ai pas les yeux en face des trous. **f.** Le moment venu, improvisez. **g.** Ça me fait chaud au cœur. **h.** Nous sommes du même avis.

3. English idioms using finger, foot, hair, and hand:

1. He has a finger in every pie. ( )

2. I cross my fingers. ( )

3. I had to put my foot down. ( )

4. He put his foot in his mouth. ( )

5. He got cold feet. ( )

6. He pulled the rug from under my feet. ( )

7. He gets in my hair. ( )

8. Give me a hand. ( )

9. He has a free hand in this. ( )

10. He was caught red-handed. ( )

11. a second-hand bookstore ( )

a. Il a le champ libre pour cela. **b.** Donne-moi un coup de main. **c.** Il m'a fallu mettre le holà. **d.** Il m'a coupé l'herbe sous les pieds. **e.** Il met son nez partout. **f.** Un magasin de livres d'occasion **g.** Il a perdu une bonne occasion de se taire. **h.** Je fais un vœu. **i.** Il me tape sur les nerfs. **j.** Il s'est dégonflé. **k.** On l'a pris la main dans le sac.

4. English idioms using head, heart, and legs:

1. He had a head start. ( )

2. I am way over my head. ( )

3. He always keeps his head. ( )

4. My heart is not in it. ( )

5. Cross my heart. ( )

6. They are pulling your leg. ( )

7. My car is on its last leg. ( )

a. Ma parole d'honneur **b.** Ma voiture est au bout de son rouleau. **c.** Je ne suis pas à la hauteur. **d.** Je n'ai pas le cœur à ça. **e.** On te fait marcher. **f.** Il avait une longueur d'avance. **g.** Il garde toujours son sang-froid.

5. English idioms using mouth, neck, nerves, and nose:

1. He is a big mouth. ( )

2. He was foaming at the mouth. ( )

3. They lived from hand to mouth. ( )

4. Put your money where your mouth is. ( )

5. Learning by word of mouth. ( )

6. He is a pain in the neck. ( )

7. I won't stick my neck out. ( )

8. You get on my nerves. ( )

9. What nerve! ( )

10. to lose one's nerve ( )

11. It's no skin off my nose. ( )

12. Don't turn your nose up (at this). ( )

13. Don't be so nosey. ( )

14. He arrived right on the nose. ( )

a. Joignez le geste à la parole. b. Je ne vais pas me mouiller. c. Il est arrivé pile à l'heure. d. Quel culot! Quel toupet! e. Tu me tapes sur les nerfs. f. Ce n'est pas mes oignons. g. De quoi je me mêle? h. Il écumait de rage. i. Il est casse-pieds/pénible. j. perdre son sang-froid k. Apprendre de bouche à oreille l. C'est une grande gueule. m. Ne faites pas la fine bouche. n. Ils vivaient au jour le jour.

6. English idioms using shoulder, skin, stomach, and tooth:

1. She gives me the cold shoulder. ( )

2. He has a chip on his shoulder. ( )

3. He has a thin skin. ( )

4. He escaped by the skin of his teeth. ( )

5. He gets under my skin. ( )

6. I was wet to the skin. ( )

7. My eyes were bigger than my stomach. ( )

8. I cannot stomach this. ( )

9. I cannot stomach him. ( )

10. to fight tooth and nail for... ( )

11. to have a sweet tooth. ( )

12. He lies through his teeth. ( )

a. Je ne peux pas digérer ça. b. Il m'énerve/Il m'exaspère. c. Il est aigri./Il en veut à tout le monde. d. Elle me bat froid. e. Je ne peux pas le blairer/le voir en peinture. f. Il ment comme il respire. g. Il a échappé de justesse. h. Défendre bec et ongles i. J'ai eu les yeux plus grands que le ventre. j. J'étais trempé jusqu'aux os. k. avoir l'épiderme sensible/être susceptible l. avoir un faible pour les sucreries

7. English idioms using throat, thumb, toes, and tongue:

1. To have a frog in one's throat ( )

2. Don't shove that idea down his throat. ( )

3. It's a cutthroat method. ( )

4. She has a green thumb. ( )

5. To be all thumbs ( )

6. As a rule of thumb ( )

7. Keep on your toes. ( )

8. From head to toe ( )

9. Don't step on her toes. ( )

10. Hold your tongue. ( )

11. I have it on the tip of my tongue. ( )

a. avoir la main verte **b.** Tenez votre langue/Bouclez-la! **c.** Restez sur vos gardes. **d.** avoir un chat dans la gorge **e.** En règle générale **f.** Je l'ai sur le bout de la langue. **g.** Voilà une méthode coupe-gorge. **h.** de la tête aux pieds. **i.** Ne lui fais pas avaler cette idée. **j.** être maladroit de ses mains. **k.** Ne lui marchez pas sur les pieds.

III. SECTION ON BUSINESS, MONEY, AND GAMBLING

1. English idioms relating to business:

1. Back to the drawing board. ( )

2. The ball is in your court. ( )

3. We burnt our bridges. ( )

4. Big deal! ( )

5. to be in the red ( )

6. All that red tape! ( )

7. Let's call it a day. ( )

8. The bottom line is... ( )

9. The project is now on the back burner. ( )

a. Ça suffira pour aujourd'hui. **b.** La belle affaire! **c.** être à découvert/en déficit **d.** Ah, la paperasserie/la bureaucratie! **e.** Retour à la case départ. **f.** On a coupé les ponts. **g.** Le projet est à présent en veilleuse. **h.** En définitive. **i.** A vous de jouer.

2. English idioms relating to money:

1. I bank on your support. ( )

2. to make big bucks ( )

3. for a lousy buck ( )

4. He made a fast buck. ( )

5. I work for peanuts. ( )

6. I am always broke. ( )

7. I paid through the nose. ( )

8. It's the other side of the coin. ( )

9. They are a dime a dozen. ( )

a. Ça m'a coûté la peau des fesses (ou les yeux de la tête). **b.** gagner du fric/s'en mettre plein les poches **c.** Je suis toujours fauché. **d.** Il y en a/On en trouve/à la pelle. **e.** Il se fait du fric facilement. **f.** C'est le revers de la médaille **g.** Je compte sur votre soutien. **h.** pour un méchant dollar/pour un misérable centime **i.** Je travaille pour des prunes.

3. English idioms relating to gambling:

1. a poker face ( )

2. You bet your life! ( )

3. to lay one's cards on the table ( )

4. When the chips are down ( )

5. lost in the shuffle ( )

6. without the ghost of a chance ( )

7. The cards are stacked against me. ( )

8. Don't push your luck. ( )

a. En fin de compte/Quand les jeux sont faits **b.** Ne joue pas avec le feu. **c.** Un visage impassible **d.** Sans l'ombre d'une chance **e.** Les dés sont pipés contre moi. **f.** Et comment! **g.** Jouer cartes sur table **h.** Perdu dans la mêlée

IV. SECTION ON CLOTHING AND COLORS

1. English idioms relating to clothing:

1. I would not like to be in your shoes. ( )

2. If..., I'll eat my hat. ( )

3. You'll lose your shirt. ( )

4. He talks through his hat ( )

5. My hat off to you!. ( )

6. We must roll up our sleeves. ( )

7. If the shoe fits, wear it. ( )

8. at the drop of a hat ( )

a. Chapeau!/Je te tire mon chapeau. **b.** Il parle à tort et à travers. **c.** ... je me fais moine/me fais pendre. **d.** à tout moment **e.** Je n'aimerais pas être dans tes pompes. **f.** Il faut retrousser nos manches. **g.** Tu y laisseras ta chemise. **h.** Qui se sent morveux se mouche.

2. English idioms relating to colors:

1. I feel blue. ( )

2. out of the blue ( )

3. He ran a red light. ( )

4. to scream blue murder ( )

5. to get the green light ( )

6. a brown-noser ( )

7. to brown-nose ( )

8. to pass with flying colors ( )

a. crier au meurtre **b.** réussir brillamment/haut la main **c.** J'ai le cafard. **d.** inopinément **e.** un lèche-bottes **f.** obtenir le feu vert **g.** faire de la lèche **h.** Il a brûlé/grillé un feu rouge.

V. SECTION ON DRINKING AND FOOD

1. English idioms relating to drinking and beverages:

1. Bottoms up! ( )

2. to be on the wagon ( )

3. Cheers!/Here's to you. ( )

4. He is off the wagon. ( )

5. He can't hold his liquor. ( )

6. to wet one's whistle ( )

7. (a drink) on the rocks ( )

8. (a drink) down the hatch ( )

9. Another round, please. ( )

10. to get drunk ( )

11. to nurse a hangover ( )

a. Il ne peut pas tenir le coup. **b.** être au régime sec **c.** Avec des glaçons **d.** Il s'est remis à picoler. **e.** prendre une cuite **f.** derrière la cravate **g.** cuver sa cuite **h.** À votre santé!/À la vôtre! **i.** Se rincer le gosier/la dalle **j.** Cul-sec! **k.** La même chose/Remettez-nous ça

2. English idioms relating to food and eating:

1. a banana republic ( )

2. to go banana/go nuts ( )

3. the Big Apple ( )

4. to bring home the bacon ( )

5. the cream of the crop ( )

6. a hot potato ( )

7. It's food for thought. ( )

8. to be in a jam ( )

9. a traffic jam ( )

10. to butter up (someone) ( )

11. a couch potato ( )

12. to spill the beans ( )

13. That takes the cake. ( )

14. icing on the cake ( )

a. faire bouillir la marmite   **b.** un sujet brûlant   **c.** un accro à la télé   **d.** la ville de New York   **e.** être dans le pétrin   **f.** la cerise sur le gâteau   **g.** le dessus du panier   **h.** vendre la mèche   **i.** passer la pommade à (qqn)   **j.** C'est le bouquet/le pompon.   **k.** Ça donne à réfléchir   **l.** un embouteillage/un bouchon   **m.** une république bananière   **n.** péter les plombs/devenir dingue

VI. SECTION ON FURNITURE AND HOUSEHOLD

1. to sweep under the rug ( )

2. to roll out the red carpet for ( )

3. I saw the writing on the wall. ( )

4. a skeleton in the closet ( )

5. a drop in the bucket ( )

6. to kick the bucket ( )

7. born with a silver spoon in his mouth ( )

8. call a spade a spade ( )

9. to treat someone like a doormat ( )

10. (a plan) It went to pot. ( )

11. (a person) He is going to pot. ( )

12. from the frying pan into the fire ( )

13. to put one's foot in the door ( )

14. to have a lot on one's plate ( )

a. casser sa pipe **b.** mettre le pied dans la porte **c.** appeler un chat un chat **d.** avoir du pain sur la planche **e.** balayer sous le tapis **f.** dérouler le tapis pour... **g.** une goutte d'eau dans la mer **h.** C'est tombé à l'eau. **i.** Je me suis rendu à l'évidence. **j.** Il se laisse aller. **k.** un cadavre dans le placard **l.** tomber de Charybde en Scylla/aller de mal en pis **m.** né dans la soie/dans du coton/né sous une bonne étoile **n.** traiter (qq'un) comme un chien

VII. SECTION ON HEALTH AND SPORTS

1. English idioms relating to health:

1. He is alive and kicking. ( )

2. to look the picture of health ( )

3. to be under the weather ( )

4. to be in tip-top shape ( )

5. to be pushing up daisies ( )

6. to be on one's last leg ( )

7. a bitter pill to swallow ( )

8. to kick the bucket ( )

9. to pull through ( )

10. He is hard of hearing. ( )

a. casser sa pipe **b.** être au mieux de sa forme **c.** respirer la santé **d.** manger les pisse-en-lit par la racine **e.** en pleine forme **f.** être au bout de son rouleau **g.** Il est dur d'oreille. **h.** une pilule difficile à avaler **i.** ne pas être dans son assiette **j.** s'en tirer/s'en sortir

2. English idioms relating to sports:

1. to get back in the game (   )

2. The ball is in your court. (   )

3. to keep the ball rolling (   )

4. to set the ball rolling (   )

5. to hit a snag (   )

6. to hit below the belt (   )

7. to be on the ball (   )

8. She plays hard ball (   )

9. It beats me. (   )

10. He calls the shots. (   )

11. to throw in the towel (   )

12. No sweat (   )

13. You are off base. (   )

14. There is a snag. (   )

15. The project is on target. (   )

16. He is a big shot. (   )

17. to take a rain check (   )

18. It's a whole new ball game. (   )

19. It's a catch--22 situation. (   )

20. the front runner (   )

a. jeter l'éponge   b. faire avancer les choses   c. le grand favori
d. tomber sur un os   e. Il y a un hic.   f. rentrer dans la danse   g. C'est une autre paire de manche.   h. C'est le serpent qui se mord la queue.
i. Pas de souci/Pas de problème   j. Elle ne fait pas de cadeaux.
k. Vous n'y êtes pas./Vous êtes dans l'erreur.   l. Ça me dépasse.   m. Il mène la danse.   n. La balle est dans ton camp.   o. remettre à une autre fois   p. C'est un gros bonnet/un gros ponte.   q. Ça se déroule comme prévu.   r. mettre les choses en route   s. être à la hauteur de la situation
t. faire un coup bas

VIII. SECTION ON NATURE, TIME, AND RELIGION

1. English idioms relating to nature:

1. a breath of fresh air. ( )

2. to be in hot (deep) water ( )

3. to beat around the bush ( )

4. a drop in the bucket ( )

5. to gain/lose ground ( )

6. Rain or shine... ( )

7. Can't see the forest for the trees ( )

8. to be down-to-earth ( )

9. to go with the flow ( )

10. to weather a storm ( )

a. une bouffée d'oxygène.   b. C'est l'arbre qui cache la forêt.
c. affronter la tempête   d. une goutte d'eau dans la mer   e. tourner autour du pot   f. suivre le mouvement   g. gagner/perdre du terrain
h. avoir les pieds sur terre   i. être dans de sales/beaux draps   j. Qu'il pleuve ou qu'il vente...

2. English idioms relating to time:

1. Better late than never. ( )

2. a race against the clock ( )

3. in the long run ( )

4. in my own sweet time ( )

5. Time is ripe. ( )

6. at the eleventh hour ( )

7. to have the time of your life ( )

8. Never in a million years. ( )

9. to lose track of time ( )

10. It's about time. ( )

11. time after time ( )

12. in the nick of time ( )

13. to play for time ( )

14. Let's call it a day. ( )

15. to serve time ( )

16. You've made my day. ( )

17. Go ahead, make my day!. ( )

18. to beat the clock ( )

19. to stand the test of time ( )

20. Long time no see. ( )

a. Restons-en là. **b.** quand bon me semble/à mon rythme. **c.** ça faisait un bail/une éternité. **d.** s'amuser comme un fou **e.** résister à l'épreuve du temps **f.** Il est grand temps. **g.** Mieux vaut tard que jamais. **h.** finir en avance **i.** purger sa peine **j.** Tu m'as mis du baume au cœur. **k.** Jamais de la vie. **l.** Vas-y, fais-moi plaisir! **m.** in extremis/juste à temps **n.** à maintes reprises **o.** C'est le moment ou jamais. **p.** chercher à gagner du temps **q.** à la dernière minute/au dernier moment **r.** perdre la notion du temps **s.** une course contre la montre **t.** à la longue

3. English idioms relating to religion:

1. to act high and mighty ( )

2. the almighty dollar ( )

3. It's hot as hell. ( )

4. He is going to catch hell. ( )

5. to raise hell ( )

6. to scare the hell out of (someone) ( )

7. Get the hell out of here. ( )

8. a blessing in disguise ( )

9. When hell freezes over ( )

10. Speak of the devil… ( )

11. It's gospel truth. ( )

12. to preach to the choir ( )

13. I have been to hell and back. ( )

14. to be in limbo ( )

a. être comme l'oiseau sur la branche **b.** C'est parole d'évangile. **c.** à la Saint-Glinglin/quand les poules auront des dents. **d.** Fiche-moi le camp/Casse-toi. **e.** Il va se faire engueuler. **f.** se donner de grands airs **g.** prêcher à des convertis **h.** un bien pour un mal **i.** Quand on parle du loup, on lui voit la queue. **j.** J'en ai vu de toutes les couleurs. **k.** Il fait une chaleur d'enfer. **l.** ficher la trouille/la frousse à (qqn) **m.** le tout-puissant dollar **n.** tempêter/faire une scène

IX. SECTION ON MUSIC AND TRAVEL

1. English idioms relating to music:

1. It's music to my ears. ( )

2. to blow/toot one's horn ( )

3. to fine tune (a project) ( )

4. It rings a bell. ( )

5. to know the score ( )

6. He plays second fiddle. ( )

7. ... and all that jazz. ( )

8. to face the music ( )

9. to blow the whistle on... ( )

10. to play it by ear ( )

11. It sounds like a broken record. ( )

a. C'est un sous-fifre. **b.** On dirait un disque rayé. **c.** affronter la tempête **d.** peaufiner/fignoler **e.** Ça me met du baume au cœur. **f.** improviser sur le moment **g.** ... et tout le bazar./et tout le bataclan. **h.** Ça me dit/rappelle quelque chose. **i.** vendre la mèche sur... **j.** se faire mousser **k.** connaître la chanson/la musique

2. English idioms relating to travel:

1. a Sunday driver ( )

2. to be a backseat driver ( )

3. the designated driver ( )

4. to drive a hard bargain ( )

5. the fifth wheel ( )

6. to hit the road ( )

7. to rock the boat ( )

8. to take someone for a ride ( )

9. My way or the highway ( )

10. to be on the wagon ( )

11. to miss the boat ( )

12. off the beaten track ( )

13. to put the pedal to the metal ( )

14. You drive me up the wall. ( )

15. to get the show on the road ( )

16 to hitch a ride ( )

17 to sail through an exam ( )

a. hors des sentiers battus **b.** rater le coche/laisser passer une occasion **c.** mener (qqn) en bateau **d.** faire du stop **e.** réussir (à un examen) haut la main **f.** C'est ça ou rien./C'est comme ça et pas autrement. **g.** être au régime sec **h.** être dur en affaires/négocier ferme **i.** Tu me fais grimper aux rideaux. **j.** un conducteur du dimanche **k.** passer à l'action   **l.** prendre la route   **m.** appuyer sur le champignon   **n.** faire la mouche du coche   **o.** faire des vagues/des histoires   **p.** la cinquième roue du carrosse   **q.** le conducteur désigné

X. SECTION ON MISCELLANEOUS IDIOMS

(presented alphabetically by keywords)

1. From A to G:

1. to be better/worse off ( )

2. to be in a bind ( )

3. to pass the buck ( )

4. The buck stops here. ( )

5. to bridge the gap ( )

6. It's a cinch. ( )

7. at six o'clock-ish ( )

9. It was an eye-opener. ( )

10. He always find fault with... ( )

11. Get your act together. ( )

12. He got cold feet. ( )

13. to get a kick out of... ( )

14. to get up on the wrong side of the bed ( )

15. Give it a shot. ( )

16. I'll give him a piece of my mind. ( )

17. a gut feeling ( )

a. Ici commence la responsabilité. b. se lever du pied gauche c. Il trouve toujours à redire à... d. éprouver un sacré plaisir à... e. J'ai eu un pressentiment/une intuition f. Il s'est dégonflé. g. combler le fossé h. C'était une révélation. i. être mieux loti/plus mal loti j. Je vais l'engueuler/lui passer une engueulade. k. C'est du gâteau! l. tente le coup. m. être dans le pétrin n. sur les six heures o. Mets de l'ordre à/dans... p. renvoyer la balle/refiler la responsabilité

2. From H to M:

1. He has no clue. ( )

2. I have it up to here. ( )

3. Home, sweet home. ( )

4. the ins and outs of... ( )

5. He jumped the gun. ( )

6. to keep track of ( )

7. I know the ropes. ( )

8. He let off steam. ( )

9. for the long haul ( )

10. Hard to make ends meet ( )

11. to have mixed feelings ( )

a. Difficile de joindre les deux bouts. b. Il n'en a pas la moindre idée. c. Je connais les ficelles. d. surveiller/garder la trace de e. Il a agi prématurément/trop vite f. les tenants et les aboutissants de... g. pour le long terme h. avoir des sentiments mitigés i. Ah, qu'on est bien chez soi. j. Il s'est défoulé/il a relâché la pression. k. J'en ai ras le bol.

3. From N to S:

1. a needle in a haystack ( )

2. There's nothing to it. ( )

3. No way, José! ( )

4. off the beaten track ( )

5. Out of sight, out of mind. ( )

6. to rip (someone) off ( )

7. run-of-the-mill ( )

8. to arrive safe and sound ( )

9. to set the record straight ( )

10. made from scratch ( )

11. Shame on you! ( )

12. the spitting image of his father ( )

13. On second thought... ( )

14. to be sick and tired of... ( )

15. It slipped my mind. ( )

16. Stand your ground. ( )

a. hors des sentiers battus **b.** Pas question!/Rien à faire! **c.** mettre les choses au clair **d.** son père tout craché **e.** Ça m'est sorti de l'esprit. **f.** Tenez bon/tenez ferme. **g.** tout à fait ordinaire **h.** une aiguille dans un tas de foin **i.** fait maison/fait à partir de zéro **j.** Quelle honte!/Tu n'as pas honte? **k.** Rien de plus facile./Rien de vrai là-dedans. **l.** Toute réflexion faite... **m.** Loin des yeux, loin du cœur. **n.** arriver sain et sauf/à bon port **o.** en avoir assez/marre de... **p.** arnaquer/

escroquer (qqn)

4. From T to Z:

1. (approval) There you go! ( )

2. to throw a fit ( )

3. to throw in the towel ( )

4. to tie the knot ( )

5. to win big time ( )

6. to owe (someone) big time ( )

7. (Something) up in the air ( )

8. You can say that again! ( )

a. se passer la corde au cou **b.** Tu l'as dit! Je ne te le fais pas dire!
c. piquer une crise/péter les plombs **d.** devoir une fière chandelle à (qqn) **e.** (qqch) d'incertain/encore vague **f.** Voilà./Très juste!
g. jeter l'éponge **h.** gagner haut la main/gagner et de loin

PART TWO

Jacques Bourgeacq

FRENCH IDIOMS

Expressions idiomatiques françaises avec leur équivalent en anglais

(French Idioms with their English equivalents)

In the course of your contacts with French, you often find yourself in the position of a listener or reader. As we have indicated earlier, French natives or near-native speakers are not always aware of the idiomatic status of all the expressions they are using instinctively in addressing their audience, so they do not always know when to adapt their level of language to foreign listeners. This is why it is important to learn to recognize or interpret such idioms whenever they reach your ears or appear in a text. This section of the book now switches to a French perspective with the general question: ***Que comprenez-vous?...*** We will now be using French in some of our explanations for your practice.

I. Sélection de comparaisons en français et en anglais:

Comparaisons (*similes* en anglais) dépendant d'un verbe:

Section 1:

Il est arrivé comme un chien dans un jeu de quilles. *He arrived like a bull in a china shop.*
– **Un jeu de quilles** is a set of bowling pins.

Il chante comme une casserole. *He can't carry a tune.*
– **Une casserole** is a cooking pan, clearly not a melodic instrument!

Je connais la ville comme ma poche. *I know the town like the back of my hand.*
– We probably see the back of our own hands more often than our palms.

Il courait comme un dératé. *He was running like hell/ like crazy.*
– **Un dératé** is someone whose spleen was removed. In ancient times, it was believed that a stitch on the side when running was caused by the spleen, so a person without a spleen could run wild without pain!

Il se débat comme un diable dans un bénitier. *He struggles like a devil in holy water.*

J'ai dormi comme un loir. *I slept like a log.*
– **Un loir** is a dormouse, known for its long hibernation. ***A log***: a 17th century English idiom, suggesting immobility.

Il entre ici comme dans un moulin. *He just waltzes in and out of here.*

– The original idiom was « ***entrer comme <u>un âne</u> dans un moulin*** ». A donkey never asks for permission!

Il est comme un coq en pâte.   *He lives the life of Riley.*
– ***Un coq en pâte*** is a culinary term referring to the aspect of a baked rooster comfortably sitting in a crust, like a pâté. An Irish-American early 20th century idiom, though nobody seems to know who Riley was!

Il fume comme un pompier.   *He smokes like a chimney.*
– Before the invention of fireproof clothing, firemen had their clothes soaked with water, which gave out vapor from the heat of the fire. The pun comes from the double meaning of ***fumer***: To smoke or to steam.

Il a joué comme un pied.   *He played like a bozo/an amateur.*
– A foot is not nearly as skilful as a hand.

Exercise: Research and provide equivalent idioms in English.

Ce costume lui va comme un gant _____

Il boit comme un trou _____

Il change d'avis comme de culotte/chemise _____

Elle chante comme un rossignol _____

Il a joué comme un dieu _____

Ils s'entendent comme chien et chat _____

Il fait noir comme dans un four _____

Section 2:

Il ment comme un arracheur   *He lies through his teeth.*
de dents.

– In the 17th century, **un arracheur de dents** was a *"rudimentary"* dentist who offered his services in public places claiming that his removal of a tooth would not hurt! ***To lie through one's teeth*** is a 13th century English expression: From the Anglo-Norman <u>Romance of Sir Guy of Warwick.</u>

Il nage comme un fer à repasser.	*He swims like a rock.*

– **Un fer à repasser**, that apparatus to iron clothes, would not float easily!

L'opération a marché comme sur des roulettes.	*The operation went like clock-work.*

– **Roulettes** are casters.

Il parle français comme un Basque espagnol.	*He speaks French like a Spanish Basque.*

– It must be remembered that the Basque population lives on both sides of the border of France and Spain. This was of course the partial point of view of the French!

Il parle français comme une vache espagnole.	*He butchers French.*

– A folk etymology deformation of the original expression above.

Il se porte comme un charme.	*He is as fit as a fiddle.*

– **Un charme** (a beech or hornbeam) is a sturdy and resistant tree. (Alternate origin: **Un charme** is also a talisman that one wears; *se porter* for a pun.) The English idiom dates back to a text by Haughton William, "*English-men for my money* " (1616). A fiddle or violin must be kept in particularly good condition.

Je m'en moque comme de ma première culotte.	*I don't give a hoot about it.*

Je m'en moque comme de l'an quarante.	*I couldn't care less about it.*

– A number of theories attempt to explain the origin of this expression. The bottom line is that the year 40 AD does not strike a relevant note in our memories, like 1776 does.

Exercise: Research and provide equivalent idioms in English.

Il jure comme un charretier _____

Il mange comme quatre _____

Il mange comme un cochon _____

Il mange comme un moineau _____

Il ment comme il respire _____

Il pleut des cordes/comme vache qui pisse _____

Ils se ressemblent comme deux gouttes d'eau _____

Il nage comme un poisson dans l'eau _____

On s'amuse comme des petits fous _____

Section 3:

Je suis comme l'oiseau　　　　　*I don't know which way to turn.*
sur la branche.
– A branch often is a very temporary station for a bird.

Il riait comme un bossu/　　　　*He was laughing his head off.*
un fou.
– Why **un bossu** (hunchback)? Laughing hard tends to bend the body forward into a curved shape.

Ils se battent comme　　　　　*They fight like cats.*
des chiffonniers.
– In ancient times, paper was exclusively produced from old rags. The **chiffonniers** (*ragmen*) collected them from house to house to sell them to paper makers. As competition was stiff, the **chiffonniers** often fought fiercely among themselves over such rags.

Ils sont comme cul et chemise.　　*They are almost joined at the hip/*
　　　　　　　　　　　　　　　They are buddy-buddy.
– Those two "*things*" live in perpetual contact with each other, as

shirtails must have been longer than they are today!

Sa remarque est tombée comme un cheveu sur la soupe.   *It came like a bolt out of the blue.*
- Hair is not always the cleanest part on the body, especially in olden days. Nor is soup the expected place for it.

Il me traite comme un chien.   *He treats me like a dog/like dirt.*

Il tremblait comme une feuille.   *He was shaking in his boots.*

Ce produit se vend comme des petits pains.   *This product sells like hot cakes.*
- The original French expression was « **comme du pain** ». It apparently refers to the biblical episode of the multiplication of the loaves of bread by Jesus. **Petits pains** are easier to sell than large loaves. An early American expression of uncertain origin, **hot cakes** was originally a synonym of *pancakes* or *waffles*.

Exercise: Research and provide equivalent idioms in English.

Ils sont comme les deux doigts de la main _____

On est serrés comme des sardines _____

Il travaille comme un fou _____

II. Proverbes français

Un proverbe est une courte phrase, souvent métaphorique, et qui offre un conseil ou une vérité pratique et de bon sens. Considérés dans leur ensemble, les proverbes forment une immense somme de sagesse populaire, qui a été transmise de génération en génération à travers les siècles. Ils ont souvent une portée universelle, ou du moins multi-culturelle, puisque certains proverbes sont identiques d'un pays à l'autre. D'autres proverbes (la plupart) diffèrent dans les images utilisées, tout en gardant la même signification.

Note: Bien que les proverbes soient moins employés aujourd'hui qu'autrefois, il est important de savoir au moins qu'ils existent et de les comprendre lorsque quelqu'un les emploie dans la conversation ou dans un texte. Et (pourquoi pas?) d'en employer un vous-même de temps en temps, lorsque l'occasion est propice...

De nombreux proverbes, du fait qu'ils ont été conçus longtemps avant l'époque moderne (p. ex. au Moyen-Age, ou même transmis du latin ou de la Bible), présentent souvent une syntaxe et un vocabulaire archaïques:

1) inversion de l'adverbe: « Mieux vaut... » au lieu de « Il vaut mieux... »;

2) absence d'article: *"Chose promise, chose due."*;

3) ellipse du pronom: « Qui dort dîne », au lieu de « Celui qui dort dîne »;

4) ellipse du verbe: « Tel père, tel fils », au lieu de « Un fils est tel que son père. »

5) inversion syntaxique: « Rira bien qui rira le dernier, » au lieu de

« Celui qui rira le dernier rira bien ».

6) verbes à valeur omni-temporelle: « L'espoir fait vivre » (maintenant et toujours)

7) fréquentes locutions impersonnelles, à sens général: « Il n'y a pas de fumée sans feu »; "<u>on</u>" comme sujet de verbes; emploi de l'infinitif au lieu de l'impératif, etc.

8) parfois rime et rythme: « Qui va à la ch*asse* perd sa pl*ace* ».

Afin de faciliter la connaissance de ces proverbes, nous ne voulons pas vous donner les solutions « *sur un plateau* ». Nous vous invitons donc à participer à **un exercice** qui consistera d'abord à **comprendre** ces expressions, puis à **expliquer** leur signification, et enfin à **proposer un proverbe équivalent** (ou parfois même plusieurs), appartenant au corpus de proverbes traditionnels de la langue anglaise.

Note: L'internet est une riche source d'information sur la signification et l'origine de ces proverbes:

www.phrases.org.uk/meanings/proverbs.html

www.france-pittoresque.com/spip.php?rubrique888

Pour vérifier vos solutions, nous avons placé en **annexe**, à la fin de ce livre, les équivalents anglais des proverbes français que nous proposons dans l'exercice ci-dessous.

Exercise de compréhension:

Reverting momentarily to English for the sake of added clarity, let's choose an example:

Chacun voit midi à sa porte.

Explanation: Before the invention of clocks, people told time by looking at the position of the sun in the sky, or with a sundial located ***near one's door***. In abstract terms, this proverb means that everyone is best familiar with one's own situation and circumstances, and therefore has his/her own privileged vantage point.

Possible equivalents: ***Everyone has his own way of doing things***, ***Everyone sees the world his own way***, or ***To each his own***. And reversing the search (now from English to French) we find that ***To each his own*** can indeed be ***Chacun voit midi à sa porte*** (for matters of opinions), and also *À chacun ses goûts* (for matters of taste).

Chaque proverbe de cette liste est accompagné d'un *indice* en anglais pour vous aider à mieux comprendre et interpréter sa signification.

Proverbes	**Indices**
Aide-toi, le ciel t'aidera.	Avoid passivity: do your part
A la guerre comme à la guerre.	Rational and wise reaction to crisis
Après la pluie le beau temps.	Hope and think positively
Aux grands maux les grands remèdes.	Choosing appropriate solutions
Bien faire et laisser braire/laisser dire.	Stay the course regardlessly...
Bien mal acquis ne profite jamais.	*un bien*, meaning a possession
Ce que femme veut, Dieu le veut.	About woman's will!
C'est au pied du mur qu'on voit le maçon.	Show us!
C'est en forgeant qu'on devient forgeron.	Observing is not enough
Chacun pour soi, et Dieu pour tous.	Individualistic principle
Charité bien ordonnée commence par soi-même.	A matter of priority
Chien qui aboie ne mord pas.	Talk is no action
Chose promise, chose due.	Keeping your word
Comme on connaît ses saints, on les honore.	Treat people by their merit
Comme on fait son lit on se couche.	Responsibility for your actions
Deux capitaines font chavirer la barque.	Only one in command

Jacques Bourgeacq

Proverbes	**Indices**
Faute avouée est à moitié pardonnée.	From contrition to forgiveness
Faute de grives on mange des merles.	Resigning oneself; *faute de*, meaning *for lack of*
Honni soit qui mal y pense.	Think no evil
Il faut battre le fer pendant qu'il est chaud.	Of smithing and opportunity
Il faut se méfier de l'eau qui dort.	Trusting stagnant water?
Il faut tourner sept fois sa langue dans sa bouche avant de parler.	Delay and think first.
Il ne faut pas mélanger les torchons et les serviettes.	Social or professional differentiation
Il ne faut pas mettre tous ses œufs dans le même panier.	Diversify
Il ne faut pas vendre la peau de l'ours avant de l'avoir tué.	Dream is not reality
Il n'y a pas de fumée sans feu.	Suspicion
Il n'y a pas de sot métier, mais de sottes gens.	Here *sot* means stupid or useless)
Il n'y a que la vérité qui blesse.	Truth and susceptibility
L'avenir appartient à ceux qui se lèvent tôt.	Ambition and action
L'espoir fait vivre.	Good for the morale
L'habit ne fait pas le moine.	Appearance and reality
L'homme propose, Dieu dispose.	About human wishful thinking
L'homme propose, la femme dispose.	Interaction of the sexes
L'oisiveté est la mère de tous les vices.	Effects of idleness
La fortune sourit aux audacieux.	Reward is for the bold
La nuit porte conseil.	Wise delaying of decisions
La vengeance est un plat qui se mange froid.	Patience and opportunity

Côte à Côte 3

Proverbes	Indices
Les chiens aboient, la caravane passe.	Stay the course, unconcerned
Les bons comptes font les bons amis.	Strict accounting among friends
Loin des yeux, loin du cœur.	Love and distance
Mieux vaut prévenir que guérir.	Wisdom of being prepared
Mieux vaut tard que jamais.	Being persistent or giving up?
Mieux vaut tenir que courir.	Ownership vs. promises
Nul n'est prophète en son pays.	Whom to trust more?
On n'apprend pas à un vieux singe à faire la grimace.	Needing no coaching
On n'attrape pas les mouches avec du vinaigre.	About diplomacy
On ne peut pas être à la fois au four et au moulin.	In sequence or simultaneously
On ne fait pas d'omelette sans casser des œufs.	Necessity of sacrifice
Partir, c'est mourir un peu.	Leaving something behind
Pas de nouvelles, bonne nouvelle.	Positive lack of awareness
Pierre qui roule n'amasse pas mousse.	Advantage of sedentarism
Petit à petit, l'oiseau fait son nid.	Patience and gradual development
Plus on est de fous plus on rit.	In praise of collective fun
Qui aime bien, châtie bien.	Old method of upbringing
Qui ne dit mot consent.	Silence speaks!
Qui dort dîne.	Sparing one's energy
Qui paie ses dettes s'enrichit.	An economic paradox
Qui ne risque rien n'a rien.	About the necessity of risk
Qui se ressemble s'assemble.	Seeking one's own kind
Qui va à la chasse perd sa place.	Keeping an eye on what's yours

Jacques Bourgeacq

Proverbes	**Indices**
Qui va lentement va sûrement.	Prudence and safeness
Qui veut noyer (tuer) son chien l'accuse de la rage.	Pretext and hypocrisy
Qui vivra verra.	Wisdom in expectation
Qui vole un œuf vole un bœuf.	About gradual corruption
Quand le vin est tiré, il faut le boire.	Being accountable for one's actions
Quand on parle du loup, on lui voit la queue.	Not always the wolf
Rira bien qui rira le dernier.	Winning in the end
Rome ne s'est pas faite en un jour.	Patience when progress is slow
Seuls les imbéciles ne se trompent jamais.	So they think!
Tel père tel fils.	About family genes
Tous les chemins mènent à Rome.	Choice of methods
Toute peine mérite salaire.	Here *peine* means task, work
Toute vérité n'est pas bonne à dire.	Here *toute* plus a negation means some, not all
Un homme averti en vaut deux.	Foreseeing is an advantage
Un tiens vaut mieux que deux tu l'auras.	Ownership vs promise
Ventre affamé n'a pas d'oreilles.	Where words are ineffective
Vouloir, c'est pouvoir	The power of will

III. Expressions idiomatiques
(appelées aussi « idiotismes » en français):

Un *idiotisme* est une courte phrase ou une simple locution imagée et *figée*, ayant souvent une valeur métaphorique.

À la différence des proverbes, les expressions idiomatiques sont d'un emploi bien plus fréquent dans la conversation de tous les jours. Certaines vieillissent vite et disparaissent, d'autres naisssent, qui disparaitront un jour. Beaucoup vivent pendant des siècles. Chaque personne possède ses idiotismes préférés et en comprend beaucoup d'autres. En fait, il serait difficile de s'exprimer pendant une minute ou deux sans employer, souvent de façon inconsciente, un ou plusieurs de ces idiotismes. Selon son inspiration et son expérience, chaque génération invente donc ses propres expressions, dont certaines se transmettent à la génération suivante. C'est ce qui explique que chaque langue conserve parfois ces expressions idiomatiques pendant des siècles.

Exercice de compréhension:

Les expressions idiomatiques ci-dessous sont classées par thèmes pour mieux orienter votre recherche. Puis chaque expression est présentée en situation dans un bref contexte pour faciliter votre compréhension.

L'internet offre aussi de nombreuses ressources sur la signification et l'origine de ces idiotismes:

http://www.expressio.fr/toutes_les_expressions.php

http://www.expressions-francaises.fr/

Examples:

Se mettre en quatre *(pour quelqu'un)*

Clue: To go through a lot of trouble...

Origin: A 17th century expression with the idea of folding one's body into 4 parts.

Equivalent: **To bend over backwards/to go the extra mile/to go out of one's way**

Chercher la petite bête

Clue: To search for tiny, insignificant details...

Origin: This idiom dates back to the late 19th century, an image of monkeys searching for lice in the heads of their peers!

Equivalent: **To nitpick/to split hair**

Alternate French idiom: **Couper les cheveux en quatre**

Section 1. Comportement (Behavior)

Aussitôt dit, aussitôt fait, je n'ai donc pas attendu pour agir!

Comme j'ai bu trop de bière hier soir, j'ai **la gueule de bois** ce matin.

Il travaillait peu, car il avait **un poil dans la main**.

Ce n'est pas beau de **casser du sucre sur le dos** des absents, qui ne peuvent pas se défendre!

Laisse-moi tranquille. Arrête de **me casser les pieds**!

Quel désordre! **Une chatte n'y retrouverait pas ses petits.**

On ne peut pas discuter avec toi: tu **coupes toujours les cheveux en quatre.**

Viens m'aider. Donne-moi donc **un coup de main.**

Ça coûte moins cher de **faire du lèche-vitrine** que d'entrer dans les magasins!

Tu n'écoutais pas; *tu étais encore dans la lune.*

Au lieu d'aller à l'école, cet enfant *faisait l'école buissonnière.*

Comme c'était dimanche, j'ai *fait la grasse matinée* jusqu'à midi.

Je fais des heures supplémentaires pour *mettre du beurre dans les épinards.*

Elle n'est pas venue à notre rendez-vous. Elle m'a *posé un lapin.*

Mon patron est autoritaire; il *fait la pluie et le beau temps* dans la compagnie.

Son humeur est exécrable ce matin: il *s'est levé du pied gauche.*

Dis-moi directement ce que tu veux. Arrête de *tourner autour du pot.*

Il faut choisir; on ne peut pas *avoir le beurre et l'argent du beurre.*

Si tu continues à *faire l'andouille* au lieu d'être sérieux, je m'en vais!

Tu m'as fait *poireauter* une demi-heure! Tu ne peux donc pas arriver à l'heure?

Vous vous trompez complètement. *Vous vous mettez le doigt dans l'œil!*

Avec lui, impossible d'avoir une discussion cohérente; il *saute* toujours *du coq à l'âne.*

Il se fâche pour un oui ou pour un non, il *est* très *soupe au lait.*

Aide-moi à faire le ménage. Mets donc un peu *la main à la pâte!*

Comme il ne s'amusait pas beaucoup à la fête, il a *filé à l'anglaise.*

Il *fait de la lèche* pour mieux faire avancer sa carrière.

Pour qu'il comprenne la situation, je lui ai *mis les points sur les i.*

Comme il ne voulait pas faire face à l'ennemi, le soldat a **pris ses jambes à son cou**.

Section 2. Difficultés (Difficulty, problem):

Cette mauvaise nouvelle m'a déprimé. Maintenant *j'ai le cafard*.

Avec tous ses cours ce semestre, *il a du pain sur la planche!*

Je dois aller à l'université à pied chaque matin. ***Ce n'est pas la mer à boire.***

Distrait, je me suis cogné la tête contre la porte. ***J'en ai vu trente-six chandelles.***

Il a oublié de se présenter à l'examen. Le voilà ***dans de beaux draps!***

Les frais de scolarité ont encore augmenté. Nous **sommes** tous ***logés à la même enseigne.***

Qu'est-ce que tu me racontes là? C'est une histoire ***à dormir debout!***

On a failli avoir un accident. ***Il était moins une!***

Pendant tout ce mois de janvier, il a ***fait un froid de canard.***

Ce n'était pas la première fois qu'il plagiait sa composition, il a enfin reçu un F. ***Il ne l'a pas volé!***

Je n'arrive pas à faire démarrer ma voiture. ***Il y a quelque chose qui cloche.***

En vieillissant, il a perdu un peu de son arrogance. ***Il a mis de l'eau dans son vin.***

Déterminé à faire un scandale, ***il a mis les pieds dans le plat.***

J'ai mal dormi la nuit dernière, c'est pourquoi ce matin ***je n'ai pas les yeux en face des trous.***

Je ne suis pas dans mon assiette aujourd'hui, je dois avoir un début de grippe.

Avec le caractère colérique de cette personne, *on ne sait pas sur quel pied danser.*

Avec tout le travail qu'il reste à faire, *on n'est pas sorti de l'auberge.*

Ton petit chat n'est pas perdu. Arrête donc de *pleurer comme une madeleine.*

Il n'avait pas trouvé mon histoire amusante du tout, et *il riait jaune.*

Si vous croyez que je vais accepter cette situation, *vous vous mettez le doigt dans l'œil!*

Votre explication n'est pas du tout convaincante. *Elle est tirée par les cheveux.*

Mon salaire est insuffisant, ce qui fait que *je tire le diable par la queue.*

La nouvelle lui a donné un tel choc qu'*il est tombé dans les pommes.* Et il a fallu le ranimer.

Ce que vous me dites là est incroyable. *Je tombe des nues!*

Tous nos efforts ont été en vain. *Nous avons travaillé pour des prunes.*

Pendant la guerre, la vie était difficile. *Nous en avons vu de toutes les couleurs.*

Section 3. Conflit (Conflict):

Je ne sais pas ce que je lui ai fait. Il ne me parle plus, *il a une dent contre moi.*

Elle ne peut pas me tolérer; je ne sais pas ce que je lui ai fait. *Elle m'a dans le nez!*

Tu ne vois donc pas que tu fais la même chose? Regarde-toi! *C'est l'hôpital qui se moque de la charité.*

Je n'ai jamais encore connu une personne si méchante! **Quelle peau de vache!**

Cet enfant était difficile à élever. **Il nous a donné du fil à retordre.**

Son récent comportement a dépassé les limites de la décence. **C'est la goutte d'eau qui a fait déborder le vase.**

Connaissez-vous la loi antique du Talion? **C'est œil pour œil, dent pour dent.**

Si un inconnu vous traite avec une familiarité exagérée, vous pouvez lui répondre: **On n'a pas élevé les cochons ensemble.**

Pour vous débarrasser de quelqu'un qui vous importune extrêmement, vous pouvez lui dire: **Casse-toi!** ou **Tire-toi!**

Je ne sais pas ce que je lui ai fait, mais **il ne peut pas me voir en peinture.** Cela m'attriste beaucoup.

Section 4: Projets (Endeavors):

Ayant fait plusieurs métiers dans sa vie, **il a plus d'une corde à son arc.**

Pas de sentiment: **les affaires sont les affaires.**

Il nous faut terminer le projet d'ici la fin du mois, **coûte que coûte.**

Le policier a immobilisé le suspect **en deux temps trois mouvements.**

Je lui suis très reconnaissant: **il a fait des pieds et des mains** pour me venir en aide.

Ne nous éloignons pas du sujet: **revenons à nos moutons.**

Ah, tu n'oublies jamais ton objectif. On peut dire que **tu ne perds pas le nord.**

Cet athlète a gagné la course aisément, **les doigts dans le nez!**

Il a fait sa fortune clandestinement, *en travaillant au noir* et sans payer d'impôts.

Section 5: Sentiments et personnalité (Sentiments and personality):

On peut se demander s'il a toute sa tête, ou *une araignée au plafond!*

Vu la façon dont il la dévore des yeux, on pourrait dire qu'il a *le béguin pour elle.*

Cet ancien politicien *a le bras long* à Washington. Il est lobbyiste!

Bien qu'il soit pauvre, c'est l'homme le plus généreux que je connaisse: *il a le cœur sur la main.*

Ce garçon tombe amoureux tous les six mois. Il a *un cœur d'artichaut!*

Ils sont tombés amoureux instantanément: des deux côtés, ce fut *le coup de foudre.*

L'intrigue de ce roman est assez intéressante, mais son style *ne casse pas des briques/ne casse rien.*

Elle m'a sauvé la vie. *Je lui dois une fière chandelle.*

Je suis absolument sûr de ce que je viens de vous dire. *J'en mettrais ma main au feu!*

Il nous parle toujours de ses succès, de ses nombreux talents, de sa supérieure intelligence, de son immense fortune... Il n'arrête pas de *se faire mousser.*

Mais moi, *je me moque* de ce qu'il proclame *comme de l'an quarante.*

A notre époque, il faut être naïf pour continuer à *voir la vie en rose.*

Section 6: Situations:

En se quittant pour peu de temps, on ne dit pas *adieu*, mais **à plus/à plus tard.**

Au lieu d'acheter des livres, je les emprunte à la bibliothèque: **Ça ne mange pas de pain.**

J'ai écrit ma composition en une heure seulement. **Ce n'était pas la mer à boire.**

Tu as finalement été admis au programme de maîtrise. **Cela s'arrose!**

Tout ce travail m'a ouvert l'appétit. Si on allait **casser la croûte**?

Il a cassé sa pipe bêtement, en faisant de l'escalade en montagne.

Et voilà qu'avec sa voix cassée il se mit à chanter, et à chanter faux en plus! **C'était le bouquet!**

Sa démonstration *était cousue de fil blanc*, son objectif tout à fait évident.

Dans Candide de Voltaire, tous les protagonistes, après leurs maintes aventures, finissent **de fil en aiguille** par se trouver réunis à la fin.

Il semblerait que, de plus en plus, en politique **la fin justifie les moyens.**

Vous n'avez pas à me rembourser tout de suite votre dette. **Qu'à cela ne tienne.**

Quand la paix règnera enfin dans le monde, **ce sera la semaine des quatre jeudis.**

Parlez à voix basse: **les murs ont des oreilles.**

Personne n'a vu ce que nous venons de faire. **Ni vu, ni connu!**

Annex: Solutions des exercices

On trouvera ci-dessous les équivalents anglais des proverbes et des idiotismes français présentés dans les exercices. Ces équivalents anglais proposés ici sont ceux qui semblent s'adapter à la plupart des situations. Cependant, il y aura des cas où un autre équivalent pourrait être plus approprié. En définitive, c'est votre jugement qui déterminera la meilleure solution face à une situation précise.

I. French proverbs and their English equivalents:

Aide-toi, le ciel t'aidera. --> Heaven helps those who help themselves.
– This French proverb comes from 17th century poet Jean de La Fontaine in his fable « Le chartier embourbé » (the carter stuck in the mud), who receives this vocal advice from Hercules in the heavens.

A la guerre comme à la guerre. --> One has to make the best of things./Keep a stiff upperlip.
– A 17th century expression, and one frequently heard in France during the last world war. It means that one has to make do with limited resources. The **stiff upper lip** describes the legendary British patriotic stoicism, and its physical expression, in the face of adversity.

Après la pluie le beau temps. --> Every cloud has a silver lining.
– This proverb goes back to Latin "*Post nubila Phoebus.*" (*nubila* means cloudy; *Phoebus* is the sun god). Something unexpectedly good often follows a period of suffering. An alternate French idiom would be: *Les jours se suivent, mais ne se ressemblent pas.* The expression *silver lining* can be traced back to John Milton's poetry - 17th century.

Aux grands maux, les grands remèdes. --> Desperate times call for desperate measures.
- Already existed in Latin: "*Extremis malis extrema remedia.*"

Bien faire et laisser braire (dire). --> Do right and fear no man./ Eat, drink and be merry.
- Trust your conscience and ignore criticisms, especially from unworthy critics (**braire** is not only for the rhyme, but also the sound made by a donkey! The English version, *Eat, drink and be merry*, comes from the Old Testament.

Bien mal acquis ne profite jamais. --> Ill gotten, ill spent.
- Uncertain origin. *Un bien* is a possession that will not be beneficial if ill acquired.

Ce que femme veut, Dieu le veut. --> A woman's will is God's will.
- Uncertain origin. The will of a woman succeeds, as if by the will of God!

C'est au pied du mur qu'on voit le maçon. --> The tree is known by its fruit/Put your money where your mouth is/The proof is in the pudding
- Uncertain origin. Talk is cheap, so show me how you build the wall! The original English version was: "*The proof of the pudding is in the eating*," which seems more logical.

C'est en forgeant qu'on devient forgeron. --> Practice makes perfect.
- Unknown origin, though it already existed in the 15th century, when smithing was an important trade.

Chacun pour soi, et Dieu pour tous. --> Every man for himself and the devil take the hindmost./Every man for himself and God save us all.
- A maxim in favor of individualism over communitarianism. It can sometimes also be the equivalent of "*Run for your life.*"

Charité bien ordonnée commence par soi-même. --> Charity begins at home.

– Another individualist medieval adage. It may also have a positive interpretation, if the judgment about charity begins with self-introspection. It was already known in the Middle Ages.

Chien qui aboie ne mord pas. --> A barking dog seldom bites/To be all bark and no bite
– The 1814 edition of the Dictionnaire de l'Académie Française states the existence of this proverb. It means that voicing one's hostility is already letting steam out, preventing an explosion and action!

Chose promise, chose due. --> A promise is a promise/Promises are made to be kept
– Already attested in the 17th century.

Comme on connaît ses saints, on les honore. --> Treat each person according to his/her merit.
– Uncertain origin, but the cult of saints was a customary practice in French medieval Catholic society. Another expression centered on saints is « *Il ne savait pas à quel saint se vouer* », meaning not knowing which way **to turn to** for help when in difficulty. *Se vouer* means to dedicate oneself.

Comme on fait son lit on se couche. --> As you make your bed you must lie in it./You made your bed, you lie in it.
– This medieval expression was « Qui fait mal son lit, mal couche et gît ». The current expression can be both a reproach or a piece of advice.

Deux patrons (capitaines) font chavirer la barque --> Too many cooks spoil the broth.
– The origin of this French idiom is unknown. The English equivalent dates back at least to the 16th century.

Faute avouée est à moitié pardonnée. --> A fault confessed is half redressed.
– Of uncertain origin. From confessed in French to forgiven in English. Note also the rhyming of both verbs.

Faute de grives on mange des merles. --> Beggars can't be choosers/Half of a loaf is better than none
– *Faute de* means for lack of. Apparently, a thush was more tasty

or tender than a blackbird... The *grive* has been known for a long time for its diet of grapes. There was another saying: « *soûl* (drunk) *comme une grive* ».

Honni soit qui mal y pense. --> Shame on whoever thinks badly of it.
- A sentence uttered by Edward III, 14th century king of England, when French was the language of the court. A legend has it that the king's daughter-in-law was mocked for having dropped her garter while dancing with him. He is said to have placed the garter on his own leg, and stopped the laughter with this very sentence. Still written in French today, it is the motto of the British chivalric Order of the Garter, founded by that king.

Il faut battre le fer pendant qu'il est chaud. --> Strike while the iron is hot/Make hay while the sun shines
- A 16th century expression, at the time when smithing was a frequent need: Seize the opportunity while it lasts.

Il faut se méfier de l'eau qui dort. --> Still water runs deep/Got to watch the quiet ones
- Another French medieval idiom: silence may hide threat or danger. The English equivalent can be either positive or negative: Silence is no sign of empty-headedness. *Still water* on the surface may hide strong currents underneath...

Il faut tourner sept fois sa langue dans sa bouche avant de parler. --> Think twice before you speak/Think long and hard before speaking/Count to ten...
- A biblical proverb: Think before you speak. Seven times? Seven is a magic number found in many expressions (seven colors of the rainbow, seven capital sins, seventh heaven, etc.).

Il ne faut pas mélanger les torchons et les serviettes. --> Separate the sheep from the goats/with goats/the wheat from the chaff
- The French idiom dates back to the 17th century, when the aristocrats ate with napkins and the servants with dish cloths (« torchons »). The English versions are from the New Testament.

Il ne faut pas mettre tous ses œufs dans le même panier. -->

Don't put all your eggs in one basket.
- This saying is apparently found in Cervantes' Don Quixote, from the 16th century.

Il ne faut pas vendre la peau de l'ours avant de l'avoir tué. --> Don't count your chickens before they hatch.
- From the fables of Aesop, and La Fontaine in French (about the bear). Also from the 16th century English poet Thomas Howell (about the chickens). The lesson is to wait for facts before judging and acting.

Il n'y a pas de fumée sans feu. --> There is no smoke without fire.
- A medieval idiom in both languages, meaning there is suspicion about a situation with only slim evidence.

Il n'y a pas de sot métier, mais de sottes gens. --> There is no foolish job, only foolish people.
- *Sot* is from the Latin sottus, meaning foolish. Here, *sot* means foolish or useless. The general meaning is that the simple jobs and those who do them are useful, and thus worthy of respect and dignity.

Il n'y a que la vérité qui blesse. --> The truth hurts.
- Of uncertain origin. When it is right on target, deep down we know a reproach addressed to us is deserved. It stresses what we repressed.

L'avenir appartient à ceux qui se lèvent tôt. --> The early bird catches the worm.
- This French expression was popularized in the 19th century before the invention of electricity, when early risers had the opportunity of working longer hours for better wages. The English version is more colorful, and was already recorded in the 17th century in John Ray's A collection of English proverbs.

L'espoir fait vivre. --> Man lives by hope.
- A straightforward and obvious proverb of popular origin in both languages. It was already in use the Middle Ages.

L'habit ne fait pas le moine. --> You can't judge a book by its cover.
- The French is a medieval saying alluding to the ill repute of certain

monks, as a lesson to beware of appearances. The English version dates back to the 1940 edition of the <u>African Journal American Speech</u>.

L'homme propose, Dieu dispose. --> Man proposes, God disposes.
– In both languages, a medieval idiom regarding unexpected results of human endeavors, attributed to divine will.

L'homme propose, la femme dispose. --> Man proposes, woman disposes.
– In both languages, a 19th century parody of the previous proverb attributed to the French writer Jules Renard in his <u>Journal</u> (1893-98). It relates to the theme of seduction.

L'oisiveté est la mère de tous les vices. --> Idleness the mother of all vices/Idle hands are the Devil's workshop
– This proverb, in its various forms and languages, is as old as antiquity and the Bible (Ecclesiastes and Proverbs).

La fortune sourit aux audacieux. --> Fortune favors the bold/the brave.
– Found in Virgil's epic poem <u>Aeneid</u>: "*Audaces fortuna juvat.*" In both languages, the message is that a serious action will bring success.

La nuit porte conseil. --> Let's sleep on it.
– A 16th century proverb, advising taking a time lapse for further reflexion and decision.

La vengeance est un plat qui se mange froid. --> Revenge is a dish best served cold.
– The French version is from Laclos' 18th century epistolary novel <u>Les liaisons dangereuses</u>, where vengeance is best enjoyed delayed, after reaching a cool head. Since **revenge** was a frequent theme in English Renaissance literature, the English equivalent may have originated at that time.

Les chiens aboient, la caravane passe. --> Let the world say what it will.
– The French saying is apparently of Turkish origin, meaning that

a dog's insignificant barking does not affect in the least a passing caravan. In both languages, the meaning is to let critics talk, ignore them, and keep on!

Les bons comptes font les bons amis. --> Short reckonings make lasting friendships.
– The French expression is of uncertain origin, though recorded in the 17th century. Disagreements about debts should be avoided, and must not get in the way of friendship.

Loin des yeux, loin du cœur. --> Out of sight out of mind.

Mieux vaut prévenir que guérir. --> An ounce of prevention is worth a pound of cure.
– A medieval proverb in both languages that wisely recommends prevention to minimize the effects of a problem. The English version stresses the *"economy"* of the process. The English version is actually a maxim from Benjamin Franklin.

Mieux vaut tard que jamais. --> Better late then never.
– This expression appears in 15th century French texts, and the English equivalent in 14th century England, with Chaucer.

Mieux vaut tenir que courir. --> Half a loaf is better than no bread./A bird in the hand is worth two in the bush.
– The French proverb dates back to the 17th century. The English version is from John Heywood's 1546 Book of proverbs. The bird in the hand refers to falconry; two birds in the bush are potential preys.

Nul n'est prophète en son pays. --> No one is a prophet in his own land.
– In both languages, this expression is attributed to something Jesus said in the New Testament, after returning to Nazareth and being met with mockery. It means that strangers recognize your worth better than your own people.

On n'apprend pas à un vieux singe à faire la grimace. --> There is no whore like an old whore.
– The French sayings is traced back to the mid-19th century: A monkey is naturally an expert at making faces. The English

proverb is apparently from Canadian Prime Minister John Turner, spoken in July 1984 referring to a peer! (Note: It has nothing to do with teaching old dogs new tricks, an expression often used as equivalent).

On n'attrape pas les mouches avec du vinaigre. --> **Honey catches more flies than vinegar.**
- This proverb, dating back to the 18th century in both languages, is self-evident. It is apparently of Italian origin.

On ne peut pas être à la fois au four et au moulin. --> **One can't be in two places at once.**
- This French saying refers to a medieval law in France that dictated that municipal mills and ovens were to be used consecutively, as two distinct processes. As a proverb, it dates back to the 17th century.

On ne fait pas d'omelette sans casser des œufs. --> **No pain, no gain.** (U.S.)/**Can't make an omelette without breaking eggs.** (England).
- This French expression was apparently used by 19th century writer Balzac, meaning that one must often sacrifice something to achieve a positive goal.

Partir, c'est mourir un peu. --> **To leave is to die a little.**
- This French proverb is of ancient origin, and was revitalized by a little-known poet, Edmond Haraucourt, at the end of the 19th century in his poem: « Rondel de l'adieu ». One always loses something upon leaving a place or someone behind.

Pas de nouvelles, bonne nouvelle. --> **No news is good news.**
- The origin of the French version is uncertain.

II. French idioms and their English equivalents:

1. Behavior:

Aussitôt dit, aussitôt fait./Sitôt dit, sitôt fait. --> **No sooner said than done.**
– This expression is of uncertain origin in both languages, meaning immediate implementation after speaking.

avoir la gueule de bois--> to have a hangover
– This French idiom appears to have originated in the 18th century, meaning a pasty feeling in the mouth akin to the taste of wood. The English version is a late 19th century americanism describing an after-effect feeling: "*hanging over*" from drinking.

avoir un poil dans la main --> to be a lazy-bones/an idle person
– An 18th century French expression; a hair in the hand shows a serious lack of use! The English idiom dates back to the late 16th century. If lazyness has penetrated the bones, what of the rest of the body?)

faire son beurre --> to make big bucks/to make a bundle/a pile
– The French expression's origin is uncertain, other than the fact that butter became increasingly prized over the centuries, and it almost became a social status symbol up to modern times.

foncer bille en tête --> To rush head on
– The 20th century French idiom means to rush head on without fear. **Une bille** (like boule) is slang for head; here **en tête** means ahead, forward.

casser du sucre sur le dos de quelqu'un --> To badmouth someone behind his back.
– In this French 17th century expression, *se sucrer de quelq'un* meant

to take him for a fool.

casser les pieds à quelqu'un --> to be such a pain/a pain in the neck/to get on one's nerves
- The French expression comes from 19th century slang. *Casser* meant to break or rather *to crush* (someone's feet), which can be almost as painful as a pain in the neck.

Une chatte n'y retrouverait pas ses petits. --> It's a real mess!
- French idioms about cats are usually fairly old, and this one is of uncertain origin. *Une chienne* is often a substitute in this idiom. Here, maternal instinct does not measure up to the extent of the mess!

chercher la petite bête --> To nitpick/to split hair
- In French, this is a late 19th century image of monkeys searching for lice in the head of their peers! The English idiom is in the same vein, as **nits** are lice eggs.

couper les cheveux en quatre --> Another expression for to split hair.
- A 17th century French expression for exaggerated precision; indeed the cut is not in the diameter, but in the length of the hair! No easy task, as lasers had not yet been invented!

déshabiller Pierre pour habiller Paul --> to rob Peter to pay Paul
- This idiom is said to describe the custom, in early Christianity, to transfer objects from church to church, especially clothing to dress up statues of saints. This custom was encouraged by Paul's 2nd letter to the Corinthians. The phrasing, especially in the English version, suggests criticism of this custom. The idiom also suggests precarious resources.

donner un coup de main à quelqu'un --> To give someone a hand
- A 19th century French idiom. Why *coup*? To mark the rapidity and brevity of the help, symbolized by the hand. The word *coup* is used in many French expressions to stress swiftness and suddenness.

être dans la lune --> to have one's head in the clouds
- As in the French idiom, the moon has long symbolized reverie. In

English, a different altitude symbolizes absent-mindedness.

être soupe au lait --> to have a short fuse
– Milk, used in the French idiom, is known to boil over suddenly, like a person "*blowing up*"; In the English expression, a *fuse* is a safety electrical device that burns and melts instantly under electical tension.

faire de la lèche à quelqu'un --> to suck up to someone/to brown-nose
– In both languages, the meaning is to flatter obsequiously for a favor. Originally, in the 18th century idiom, the object licked by a dog was a pair of boots, and it still exists: « **lécher les bottes à quelqu'un** ». In English, the meaning of ***brown-nose*** is clear enough.

faire du lèche-vitrine --> to go window-shopping
– In both languages, a 20th century idiom describing the "*close*" attention paid by passers-by to the show cases of stores. *Lécher* means to lick, depicting an onlooker glued to the windows.

faire la grasse matinée --> to sleep in/to sack in
– The French derives from a 15th century idiom, « dormir la grasse matinée », which can have various interpretations: ***grasse*** for the softness of the bed, and perhaps the idea that inactivity leads to fattening… **To hit the sack** is another English idiom relating to bed, and its equivalent in French would be « ***aller au plumard*** » (from ***plumes***, meaning the feathers in the mattress).

faire l'andouille --> to goof around/monkey around/horse around
– From the Latin ***inductilia***, meaning "*to be filled.*" Probably referred in medieval France to the intestinal membrane used to make sausages. An ***andouille*** is indeed a type of sausage made of tripes. *Faire* means here to pretend to be…/to act as. It's uncertain how ***andouille*** became a word used to describe clumsy humans, except if we understand it as a mildly satirical term. The equivalent varies depending on the situation. Alternate expressions: faire l'imbécile/l'idiot, etc.

faire l'école buissonnière --> to play hooky/play truant

– **Buisson** has several medieval origins, including bush, an easy place to hide. School children disinclined to attend classes found a way to skip the ordeal! In the English case, **hooky** may come from the Dutch **hoekje**, meaning nook, corner, or the game of hide and seek.

faire la pluie et le beau temps --> to call the shots
– The French idiom is an 18th century expression referring to Greek gods. It may have also been a reference to Sainte Geneviève, Catholic protective saint of Paris, who was thought to have the power to control the elements. In the English expression, the *shot* seems to refer to calling where the shot is aimed at, in a shooting range or in a game of billiards.

filer à l'anglaise --> to take a French leave/to leave unnoticed/to slip out
– Research shows how sometimes countries project their own bad behavior onto other societies. That's the case in both languages here, where the French and the English societies scored on each other! Just an example of many such cases.

mettre du beurre dans les épinards --> add a little extra to the kitty
– Over the centuries, butter increased in popularity. In the French idiom, spinach became tastier with the addition of butter.

mettre la main à la pâte --> to pitch in/to roll up one's sleeves
– A French idiom referring to a baker kneading his dough. In English, you *roll up your sleeves* (**on retrousse ses manches**) before digging your hands in the dough. Symbolically, this idiom includes also the idea of participating in a physical task, of "*pitching in.*"

mettre les points sur les i --> to dot the i's and cross the t's
– Medieval gothic handwriting made the letter **i** difficult to read, unless a dot was placed on it, in both languages. Metaphorically, the idiom means to make the message perfectly clear.

pleurer comme une madeleine --> to cry one's eyes out
– The French saying refers to Mary of Magdala, a disciple of Jesus, and a main figure of the New Testament. She appears several times in the Gospels, among them a particular episode where she shed tears of

repentance while pouring perfume on Jesus' feet.

poireauter/faire le poireau --> to cool one's heels/to wait in vain
– From the 19th century expression *planter son poireau*, an image of the straight vertical leek planted tall in the ground. Another expression, *être planté là*, seems to echo the leek image when referring to a person. It means to be standing motionless, waiting.

poser un lapin à quelqu'un --> to stand someone up
– In the 19th century, this French idiom meant refusal to pay one's debt, in particular after a sexual favor! It gradually came to mean to skip a meeting or a date. Another expression, *faire poser quelqu'un* used to mean to make someone wait.

prendre ses jambes à son cou --> to take to one's heels
– Another strange but similar 17th century French idiom, « *prendre ses jambes sur son col* », meant to go on a trip, presumably on foot. **Sur son col** referred to carrying a bag with a strap **around the neck**. A bit far-fetched indeed! Today, the expression has evolved to mean to leave precipitously, to split (slang).

sauter du coq à l'âne --> to be a scattered brain/to be all over the place
– In this French idiom, *l'âne* was not a donkey, but a mispelled or archaic **asne** (a female duck). The original 14th century idiom was « *saillir du coq à l'asne* » referring to a rooster's occasionally "*servicing*" a female duck! From this bizarre image came the idea of jumping from one topic to another without coherence or connection. Note also that the slang verb *sauter* means to copulate in certain contexts. Our ancestors had a fertile imagination!

se lever du pied gauche --> to get up on the wrong side of the bed
– The left side was already a bad omen in Latin (*sinistra* means left). Superstition about that side remained through the Middle Ages. Even today the adjective *gauche* (French for *left*, and English for *clumsy*) is a remnant of this superstition. A bad mood is often explained by this idiom.

se mettre (se fourrer) le doigt dans l'œil --> to be entirely mistaken/to bark up the wrong tree

– Although few people may be aware of it, in the Middle Ages the word *oeil* (eye) was also slang for the anus. In the English expression, the prey that was in the tree has moved away, while the dog keeps barking at it.

tourner autour du pot --> to beat around the bush
– A 14th century French idiom referring to the kettle of food during periods of famine, around which members of the family turned, hesitating to serve themselves. *Beating around the bush* is a medieval hunting practice: "*beaters*" were men flushing the birds hiding in the bush.

vouloir le beurre et l'argent du beurre --> wanting to have your cake and eat it too
– This is probably a 19th century French expression: A farmer can't sell his/her butter while still honestly keeping it. The English version is found in the 16th century texts of several English authors: John Heywood, John Davies, Thomas, Duke of Norfolk, etc. The idea is that one "*cannot have it both ways.*" There has been some debate regarding the phrasing. Why not a more logical expression such as *to eat your cake and still have it*?

2. Difficulty, problem:

avoir le cafard --> to have the blues
– Among the various meanings of *cafard*, including cockroach, snitch, hypocrite, etc., the term here refers to melancholy, spleen (archaic). The 19th century poet Charles Baudelaire uses both words, *cafard* and *spleen* in Les Fleurs du mal. *The blues* probably comes from *the blue devils*, hallucinations from withdrawal from a drunken state. It seems to also have been applied to the depressive mood of slaves and their "*singing the blues.*"

avoir du pain sur la planche --> to have a lot on one's plate
– Until the late 19th century, this French idiom meant to have enough bread on the bakery shelves for a long time. The expression was later applied to prisoners receiving bread in exchange for work. The modern idiom means to have a lot of work or commitments ahead. The English overloaded *plate* seems to be a recent idiom: an overwhelming situation!

Ce n'est pas la mer à boire --> It's not that big a deal./It's not such a big issue.
– This French idiom appears in La Fontaine's fable « *Les deux chiens et l'âne mort* » (17th century). The English version was apparently first used in Western New York at the turn of the 20th century.

en voir trente-six chandelles --> to see stars
– A 15th century expression describing the effects of a physical or psychological shock. The term **chandelles**, meaning candles, was originally used by itself. Then a quantity was added, first 1,000, then 100, and finally 36, a number often used with religious significance. In the English expression, **stars**, by their sheer numbers, can produce a dazzling luminosity on the night sky, especially before the invention of electrical lights.

être dans de beaux (sales) draps --> to be in a nice mess/in deep doo doo/up to one's eyeballs
– A medieval French idiom, whereby **draps** meant **clothes**, not sheets. Persons guilty of lust were shamed by having to attend mass in white clothes, a mortification in the style of The Scarlet Letter! Today, in this ironic idiom, **beaux draps** has the meaning of being in a precarious situation. In the English phrases, **doo doo** is a euphemism for excrements.

être logé à la même enseigne --> to be in the same boat
– In 16th century France, *l'enseigne* was the sign of a shop or an inn. Accommodations and conditions were the same for all guests. Whether in an inn or on a boat, an equal situation or treatment is the rule.

Une histoire à dormir debout* --> *a tall tale/a cock-and-bull story/a lot of bull(shit)
– The meaning of this French idiom has not changed much since the 16th century. It refers to a story so unrealistic, that one ends up falling asleep while standing, just out of boredom. For the English expression, while the meaning of **bull**, as nonsense (in old French **boul/bole**, meaning deceit, fraud) dates back to the 17th century, the modern term **bullshit**, related to the animal, has been used in America since the early 20th century. The **cock** and the **bull** were names of English inns on a long road where stagecoach travelers

used to tell extravagant stories to kill time.

Il était moins une! --> It was close!/close shave!/a close call!
– The expression *moins une* refers to time, e.g., just **one second** earlier or later a catastrophy would have happened. The English equivalents are from 18th century barber shop and sport referee talk. Other idioms are *a narrow escape, a near miss*.

Il fait un froid de canard. --> It's bitterly cold/It's cold as a witch's tit
– This French expression, of uncertain origin, comes from duck hunting, which in Europe has been practiced in the heart of winter, because ducks are easier preys in bitter cold temperatures. The hunter hides motionless, waiting for ducks, feeling the cold. For the English expression, a witch was thought to have no maternal instinct.

Il ne l'a pas volé! --> He had it coming!/He was asking for it!/Serves him right!
– The French expression seems to date back to the 19th century. It is an ironic judgment on deserved retribution.

Il y a quelque chose qui cloche. --> Something smells fishy/Something is not right
– The verb *clocher* not only meant *to be wrong*, but also *to limp*, waving like a bell. Bells were rung frequently in medieval times to announce or signal various happenings or events, including alarms.

mettre de l'eau dans son vin --> to come down a peg or two
– This French idiom can be traced to the 16th century. Cutting down alcohol content makes wine less potent and aggressive, and the drinker less demanding. Metaphorically, the idiom means *to mellow out*, to be less demanding.

mettre les pieds dans le plat --> to make a gaffe/to put one's foot in one's mouth
– Contrary to what might appear to be evident, *le plat* in this French idiom is not a dish, but a stretch of shallow water like a pond or a marsh. Wading in this clear, undisturbed water results in making it

murky. By the same token, someone who speaks about things better left unsaid commits a great disturbing gaffe, as the English says employing this French/Occitan word. *Gaffe* means a ford, a passage across. The English **foot in the mouth** idiom may refer to the foot-and-mouth disease in cattle.

ne pas avoir les yeux en face des trous --> to be unable to focus/unable to think straight
- A 17th century idiom, « *avoir les yeux de travers* », or crossed eyes, was the original expression. The modern one has a similar meaning, but it describes a lack of focus due to alcohol or lack of sleep.

ne pas être dans son assiette --> not to be one's usual self/to feel out of sorts
- In the Middle Ages, the word *assiette* meant spatial position. It referred only later to a sitting position at a table, and then to the food plate. In aviation, *assiette* is used to describe the inclination of the airplane. So metaphorically, this idiom means that one is not his/her usual, well-balanced self. ***Out of sorts*** is probably a printing expression, *sorts* being the small pieces assembled for typesetting and printing. No sorts, no printing.

ne pas savoir sur quel pied danser --> not to know where to stand/to be unsure about what to do
- A 15th century French expression that has kept its metaphorical meaning. ***Dancing*** means here deciding, acting. Dancing stresses action; standing emphasizes hesitancy, inaction.

On n'est pas sorti de l'auberge. --> We are not out of the woods yet
- A 19th century slang word: *l'auberge* was *la prison*. Metaphorically, the expression refers to an unpleasant situation with no relief expected soon. Neither is being lost ***in the woods***, part of the English expression, an uncomfortable situation. This idiom was already in use in early 19th-century America.

rire jaune --> to give a forced laugh/to laugh on the other side of one's face
- This expression probably dates back to the 18th century, and derives from hepatitis, an illness that tends to turn the skin a dull yellow and

induces bad mood in the patient. By extension, such a person is said to pretend laughing or smiling. It is the opposite of saying: "*It's not funny!*"

une explication tirée par les cheveux --> a far-fetched explanation
- A 16th or 17th century French idiom of uncertain origin. One may suggest that pulling by the hair is an easy method of forcing a person or their story to move the way you want. Metaphorically, it can describe an unbelievable or twisted story or explanation.

tirer le diable par la queue --> Live from hand to mouth/to be hanging on by one's fingernails/to struggle to make ends meet
- A 17th century French idiom with conflicting origins. The most plausible is a last resort appeal to the devil for help when in a destitute situation. The means to retain the devil? Keep grabbing him by the tail! *To make ends meet* may refer to the end of the month and the end of the savings... There's no confirmed origin for this idiom, but it might rather refer to the bottom line of an accounting sheet.

tomber dans les pommes --> to pass out/to black out/to conk out
- Apparently, this French idiom may date to the late 19th century. Its possible origin, though a bit far-fetched, may be with French writer George Sand, who used the expression « je suis dans les pommes cuites » (cooked, baked apples), i.e. feeling mushy, very tired.

tomber des nues --> to be flabbergasted/to be dumbfounded
- This 17th century French expression uses *nues*, an old term for *nuages*, to describe a person's sudden fall from a dream-like world of illusion to a concrete state of reality, often unpleasant. *Dumbfounded*, which dates back to the mid-17th century is composed of dumb and (con)found, meaning to made speechless with amazement.

travailler pour des prunes --> to work for peanuts/for chicken feed
- This French idiom relates to a 12th century story that narrates the crusaders' return from the second crusade. Back from Damascus with prune trees as their most valuable bounty, the king asked them

ironically if they had gone to the holy land *for plums*! The meaning of *pour des prunes* has stuck till this day! *Peanuts* and *chicken feed* are insignificantly small and quite cheap.

en voir de toutes les couleurs --> to go through the mill/the wringer/to have seen it all
- This French expression is of uncertain origin. It describes too much of a hard time, not only of all sorts, but of all nuances, i.e. colors. *Through the mill* may have referred to an English court, called the Mill, that heard cases of insolvency prior to bankruptcy proceedings.

3. Conflict:

avoir une dent contre quelqu'un --> To have (hold) a grudge against someone
- From a 14th century idiom: « *avoir les dents sur quelqu'un* », a sign of aggressiveness. The meaning is holding a grudge. The English term *grudge* has lost its original meaning of grumble, derived from the old French *grouchier*, having the same root as grouchy.

avoir quelqu'un dans le nez --> cannot stand someone
- Of uncertain origin, this French idiom uses smell as a sign of repulsion. There is a similar French idiom: « *Je ne peux pas le sentir* », meaning *I can't smell him*. In this context, *sentir* corresponds to the English **to stand**, meaning *to tolerate*.

C'est l'hôpital qui se moque de la charité. --> It's the pot calling the kettle black/Look who is talking
- This French expression calls attention to hypocrisy, and it refers to two real institutions in some medieval cities, e.g., Lyon: The public *hospital* and a religious series of *hospices* called *Notre-Dame de la Charité*, both welcoming the poor and the sick. One could not, of course, *scoff at*, i.e. reject, the other. The English expression *the kettle* may have been inspired by a similar expression in Cervantes' Don Quixote.

C'est une (vraie) peau de vache. --> He is a (real) bastard/a mean SOB or bitch
- A 19th century French idiom that was once an insult to the police, called *vaches*. It probably referred to the way cows will sometimes

give an unexpected kick sideways. ***Peau*** is also derogatory when it is a metonymy for a person (for example *une vieille **peau***, meaning an old hag).

donner du fil à retordre à quelqu'un --> To make life difficult for/to give someone a headache/a hard time
- A 17th century expression from the trade of weaving: « **Retordre du fil** » meant to braid or twine threads. It was a delicate manual operation, as threads were not always of the same thickness, hence the general idea of a difficult operation.

la goutte d'eau qui fait déborder le vase --> the straw that broke the camels's back/the last straw
- This French idiom already appears in 17th century literature (Mme de Sévigné): A small insignificant event can sometimes trigger grave and immediate consequences. In the English case, one may ask why a camel when there was a similar expression with ***a horse's back***. No explanation can be found, other than a possible middle-eastern origin from the colonial conquest era... There is no trace of a camel idiom in the Bible, other than a camel passing through the eye of a needle, but according to Aramaic research, the word did not mean a camel then, but a ***string***, which makes more sense!

Œil pour œil, dent pour dent. --> An eye for an eye, a tooth for a tooth.
- This idiom is found in the Bible, and it's called the **law of talion**, from the Latin **talio**, meaning retaliation. It is a very ancient law, from the Kingdom of Babylon, requiring a punishment identical to the crime. It's often invoked as a pretext for revenge.

On n'a pas élevé les cochons ensemble. --> Do I know you?
- This French expression is of uncertain origin. Raising pigs being a rather lowly occupation by upper-middle class standards, it was used to correct someone adressing you with excessive familiarity. Another expression along the same vein is « ***être copains comme cochons*** » (joined at the hip/buddy-buddy). Here, **cochons** is a corruption of the old French **soçion**, meaning associate. **Copain**, from the Latin ***cum*** and ***panis***, meant literally *"sharing bread with."*

se casser/casse-toi/se tirer/tire-toi (slang) --> to spilt/shove off/

hit the road
- In the early 19th century, a slang expression for escaping from prison was « *se casser la jambe* », a risk when jumping over a prison wall! A century later, *se casser* meant just to *take off*. The idioms *Casse-toi/Tire-toi* can be translated as *Bog off/Piss off/Scram!*

ne pas pouvoir voir quelqu'un en peinture --> cannot stand the sight of someone/cannot stomach someone
- An 18th century French expression that describes a strong dislike for not only a particular person, but even his/her portrait! The **stomach** English idiom suggests an image of indigestion!

4. <u>Endeavors</u>:

avoir le bras long --> to be well connected/to have pull
- Especially when used in the singular, a long arm, as the French expression says, is a synonym of influence, of power through a network of connections. It was already used in 17th century literature (Madame de Sévigné).

avoir plusieurs cordes à son arc --> to have more than one string to one's bow/many tricks up one's sleeves
- The original 13th century expression was « *avoir <u>deux</u> cordes à son arc* ». Then *plusieurs* replaced *deux*. The bow and the strings represent an objective to achieve and, as needed, a plurality of resources and capacities. The first English equivalent is also from the realm of war, whereas the second idiom moves to gambling, stressing a not-so-commendable, sneaky strategy!

Les affaires sont les affaires. --> Business is business
- An English expression from George Colman's 18th century comedy, <u>The Man of business</u>. The idiom states a principle, which can potentially be used to justify the means to an end. The French idiom is a literal translation from the English motto.

coûte que coûte --> at all costs/at any cost/no matter the cost/no matter what
- Not a real idiom in either language, but rather a subjunctive phrase expressing a <u>hypothetical situation</u>: "*Let it cost what it will cost.*"

en deux temps trois mouvements --> in a jiffy/in no time/in a matter of seconds
- This 18th century French expression described the military manner of presenting arm, i.e. *in two steps* (*deux temps*). The rest of the idiom, *trois mouvements*, was added a century later as an amplification to stress the rapidity of the action. In the first English expression, *a jiffy* was an old tiny unit of time, still used today in science and technology. For the profane, it simply means very quickly.

faire des pieds et des mains pour... --> to move heaven and earth toward...
- In the French idiom, the use of feet stresses using more than the usual means (hands) to achieve one's goal. There is an 18th century version: « *y aller des pieds et des mains/travailler des pieds et des mains* ». The current version dates back to the 19th century. The English equivalent apparently originated in ancient Egypt, where the god Amun was worshipped, and the mere mention of his name *shook the heaven and the earth*.

Revenons à nos moutons. --> Let's get back to the point/the issue.
- This is a quote from a medieval French play, La Farce de Maître Pathelin (1457). In this play, a crooked lawyer, Maître Pathelin, repeats this phrase to bring his cunning client, a humble and naive-looking shepherd, back to the topic at hand. The idiom remains alive to this date.

Ne pas perdre le nord --> To know on which side one's bread is buttered/to have one's head screwed on right
- Of uncertain origin, this French idiom probably refers to navigation by compass, and is metaphorically applied to life situations requiring a clear head. Not to be confused with *perdre le nord/perdre la boussole (compass)*, which means to lose one's head, to become insane.

réussir les doigts dans le nez --> to win hands down/standing on one's head/with flying colors
- This early 20th century French expression probably comes from horse racing, where the reporter commented on the ease with which a

jockey finished first: **Picking his nose** instead of concentrating on the challenge. How confident and carefree can you get! The first English equivalent comes also from horse racing. **Hands down** shows the same confidence as the French expression, loosening the reins and still winning! **With flying colors** originated in the Navy, when ships returned home with all their flags up, showing victory.

travailler au noir --> to moonlight/to do undeclared work
- Apparently a French translation from a German expression from the First World War, when illegal work and trade was caused by severe shortages of goods. Another theory mentions the Middle Ages, when clandestine work was done at night in the dark (*noir*). *Le marché noir* is black market, and *faire du marché noir* is to trade or buy on the black market.

5. Sentiments and personality:

avoir une araignée au plafond --> to have bats in the belfrey/a screw loose
- A 19th century far-fetched French idiom coined by Parisian prostitutes. For them, a person's strange but harmless behavior evoked spiders, which tend to weave their webs in the upper corners of ceilings. The English equivalent presents a similar image of strange occurrences in the head. The expression *a screw loose* originated from the early time of machines during the Industrial Revolution, evoking "*rattling*" in the head!

avoir le béguin pour quelqu'un --> to have a crush on/to be sweet on someone
- The name *béguin* comes from a 13th century religious movement of lay, liberal women called *béguines*, who lived in communities in Belgium. They wore a hood of fine cloth called *béguin,* that covered much of the head. *Avoir le béguin* is parallel with the expression *être coiffé de quelqu'un* (to be covered, i.e. blinded as by such a hood). Remember, love is blind!

devoir une fière chandelle à quelqu'un --> to owe someone big time/to be deeply endebted
- The French idiom probably originated in the Middle Ages, when gratitude to God or the Church was expressed with a candle lit at

an altar. *Fière* meant then important. Today the idiom can apply as well to gratitude toward a person. Used at the end of a sentence, the saying *big time* is a mid-19th century American idiom meaning extremely. It originated in the public's review of vaudeville: "*big time*" was the highest rating awarded.

avoir le cœur sur la main --> to be big-hearted/to be all heart
- From an earlier 17th-century expression, « avoir le coeur dans la main » meant to be very generous. **Sur la main**, is even more so, since the heart is thus even more open and available. The heart was then considered the seat of emotions.

avoir un cœur d'artichaut --> to be a hopeless romantic/to be fickle
- This 19th-century idiom is based on the manner in which an artichoke is often consumed: Leaves are detached from the heart and shared, as someone gives out his/her affection or love around. Basically, it means to become infatuated easily and frequently. The connotation of sharing pleads to the idea of being fickle: A movement from the center out to the perimeter. In the English idiom, the word *romantic* referring to love is more American than French.

avoir le coup de foudre pour... --> to fall head over heels for/in love at first sight
- This French expression, evoking a sudden and brutal natural event, gradually slid to the sentimental realm in the 18th century, with the meaning of sudden passion (*la foudre*, meaning lightning and fire). It is interesting that in both French and English, love is associated to *a fall. (falling for someone head over heels, tomber amoureux*). A strange expression to reach up to the seventh heaven!

Ça ne casse pas des briques./Ça ne casse rien. --> It's nothing to write home about/It's no big deal
- The phrase *des briques* may have been a corruption of *des vitres,* which is more plausible. In this case, the projectile had to be very small and light, metaphorically of little significance. The ironic expression *Big deal*! is also translated as *La belle affaire*!

en mettre sa main au feu --> **to stake one's life on it/to bet your (sweet) life**
- This idiom is from a medieval trial called <u>Le jugement de Dieu</u>, an ordeal whereby an accused person was ordered to stick his hand in a fire as a test of culpability. If no burn occurred, it was a proof of innocence. So what better guarantee is there than to cite this expression as a sign of truthfulness! Thank heaven for DNA testing!

se faire mousser --> **to blow (toot) one's own horn/to be full of oneself**
- An idiom from the early 19th century, using the image of soapy foam to stress the hollowness of certain discourse: It applies to someone exaggerating his worth or actions, that are no more than "*empty soapsuds.*" **To blow a horn** was a heraldry term: Important people had heralds to praise them. Some insignificant people sometimes were, and still are, their own herald!

s'en moquer comme de l'an 40 --> **Couldn't care less/to not give a damn/a hoot**
- This idiom comes with a number of theories, one of them stating **l'an 40** (the year 40) as a deformation of the <u>Alcoran</u> (the Coran). Whichever theory would prevail, the basic idea is that this particular, far remote year has no real meaning or historical importance. Another expression is « ***se moquer comme de sa première culotte*** » (like caring about your first pants). A ***dam*** was the currency of India before the rupee; ***a damn*** is thus a corruption of the original expression. ***A hoot*** is the cry of an owl. Why a hoot for caring?

voir la vie en rose --> **to see life through rosy glasses/everything through rose-colored glasses**
- This expression began in the early 19th century, and was popularized further in 1945 with Edith Piaf's famous song « La vie en rose ». The color ***rose*** (pink) symbolizes an optimistic or romanticized view of life. The rose color is symbolic of bliss and unconditional love.

6. <u>Situations</u>:

À plus
- A colloquial abreviation for *À plus tard*, meaning *See you later*.

Ça ne mange pas de pain. --> No harm in trying/it does not cost much/can't hurt
- A 17th century French expression using the food staple of the time as a metaphor: As long as the situation was not negatively affected, it was fine to proceed with any action as desired.

Ce n'est pas la mer à boire. --> It's no big deal/It's not such a big issue
- From a 17th century fable by Jean de la Fontaine, « Les deux chiens et l'âne mort », two dogs undertake to drink a lake dry in order to gain access to a floating prey, unaware of such an impossible task.

Cela s'arrose!/Il faut fêter ça!/--> It calls for a celebration
- From the root *ros*, meaning dew, the verb ***arroser*** means to pour liquid on something, usually water. But in the current context, an alcoholic beverage will celebrate much better a joyous occasion. Alcohol often has a social function and symbolic meaning.

casser la croûte --> To have a bite to eat/a snack
- A 19th century French idiom alluding to bread, essential food among the French. In France, the tradition is for breaking, rather than cutting bread, and is probably derived from the Eucharistic rite in the New Testament. It stands for the general meaning of eating, since bread is an essential part of the meal.

casser sa pipe --> to kick the bucket/to conk out/to croak
- This French idiom already existed in the 17th century, though the origin of its meaning is uncertain. Symbolically, the pipe stands for its owner, and death corresponds to the breaking of the pipe. In the case of the first English expression, there are several theories about **kicking the bucket**, the main one implying self-hanging, and none confirmed by facts.

C'est le bouquet! --> That caps it all!/That takes the cake!
- Already in the 18th century this French expression used a term describing the grand finale of a display of fireworks, called ***le bouquet***. The idiom is used ironically to condemn an unpleasant situation by pointing to what it is not: Splendid! In the second English expression, ***that takes the cake*** is an ancient expression that

entered the language in the 19th century: A cake was the prize for winning a competition.

cousu de fil blanc --> obvious/utterly predictable/doesn't hold water
- Already known in the 16th century, this French expression was derived from sewing: *To baste, to sew temporarily.* This stitch, most often white, is visible. Metaphorically, this idiom points to a story or an explanation <u>obviously</u> unbelievable. The third English expression is of uncertain origin, **to hold** or **not to hold water** referred to the reliability of the container.

de fil en aiguille --> one thing leading to another
- Borrowed from the realm of sewing in the 13th century, this French expression has been applied since to describe a progressive change of situation or topic, as thread (*fil*) slides through the eye of a needle (*aiguille*).

La fin justifie les moyens. --> The end justifies the means.
- In both languages, a famous immoral principle from 16th century's Niccolò Machiavelli's <u>The Prince</u>, justifying any method toward achieving success.

Qu'à cela ne tienne. --> Never mind/No matter/Whatever
- A 17th century French expression minimizing the difficulty of a problem. *Tenir à* expresses connection, meaning to be tied to. Literally translated is **let it be tied only to that**... In other words, the connection is of little importance or consequence.

la semaine des quatre jeudis --> When hell freezes over.
- Already in the 15th century this French expression pointed to Thursday, a day of rest for school children and a Catholic "*fat*" day, that is, a day when eating meat was OK, unlike Friday. Thursday was thus a very desirable day! From three originally, the idiom switched to four Thursdays!

Les murs ont des oreilles. --> (The) walls have ears./Loose lips sink ships.
- A 17th century French idiom recommending caution in speaking out loud for fear of being heard by hostile or indiscrete ears. The second

English idiom, ***loose lips sink ships*** was used in WWII, calling for discretion regarding the risk of enemy ears.

Ni vu, ni connu. --> What the eye doesn't see (the heart does not grieve over)!
– An 18th century exclamation of pleasure and relief in French for having done unnoticed a less-than-commendable deed.

A Brief Bibliography:

Ammer, Christine, <u>The American Heritage Dictionary of Idioms</u>, Houghton Mifflin Company, 1997.

Bibard, Frédéric, <u>365 Days of French Expressions</u>, CreateSpace Independent Publishing Platform, 2014.

Cassagne, Jean-Marie, <u>101 French Idioms</u>, Passport Books, 1995.

Lupson, P. and Pélissier, M.L., <u>Guide to French Idioms</u>, Passport Books, 1987.

Terban, Marvin, <u>Scholastic Dictionary of Idioms</u>, Scholastic, Inc., 1996.

Internet websites consulted:

"The Phrase Finder":
www.phrases.org.uk/meanings/proverbs.html

« La France Pittoresque »:
www.france-pittoresque.com/spip.php?rubrique888

« Les expressions françaises décortiquées »:
http://www.expressio.fr/toutes_les_expressions.php

« Expressions françaises »:
http://www.expressions-francaises.fr/

Reverso Bottom of Form "*Reverso*"
http://dictionnaire.reverso.net/francais-definition

Oxford Dictionary of English Idioms - Oxford Reference
www.oxfordreference.com/view/10.1093/acref

Idiom Site List & Essential Idioms - Learn English Have Fun
www.learn-english-have-fun.com/idiom-site.html

Other Books

by Virginia Institute Press

Communicative Focus: Teaching Foreign Language on the Basis of the Native Speaker´s Communicative Focus, 2nd Edition, Boris Shekhtman – June 2015

Côte à côte 1: Étude comparative de l'anglais et du français (French/English), Jacques Bourgeacq – November 2015

Côte à côte 2: Le français tel qu'on le pense, Eléments de grammaire, de stylistique et de lexicologie, Jacques Bourgeacq – September 2017

Diagnostic Assessment at the Superior/Distinguished Threshold, Bella Cohen – January 2015

The Gospel of Damascus (Arabic, French and Spanish language fiction), Omar Imady – November 2016

How to Improve Your Foreign Language IMMEDIATELY, 3rd Edition. Foreign Language Communication Tools, Boris Shekhtman – January 2014

Individualized Study Plans for Very Advanced Students of Foreign Language, Betty Lou Leaver – March 2017

Poemas y Laberintos/Poems and Labyrinths (Spanish/English poetry), Idy Linares – May 2015

Sonría y aprenda/Smile and Learn (Spanish/English – reading, comprehension, and vocabulary building), Idy Linares – September 2014

What Works: Helping Students Reach Native-Like Second-Language

Competence, 2nd Edition. Rocío Txabarriaga, editor. Authorial collective: Rajai Rasheed Al-Khanji, James Bernhardt, Gerd Brendel, Tseng Tseng Chang, Dan Davidson, Christian Degueldre, Madeline Ehrman, Surendra Gambhir, Jaiying Howard, Frederick Jackson, Cornelius Kubler, Betty Lou Leaver, Maria Lekič, Natalia Lord, Michael Morrissey, Boris Shekhtman, Kenneth Shepard, Svetlana Sibrina – May 2015

Working with Advanced Foreign Language Students, 2nd Edition, Boris Shekhtman – March 2016

www.virginiainstitutepress.com

Côte à Côte 3

www.ingramcontent.com/pod-product-compliance
Lightning Source LLC
Chambersburg PA
CBHW070639050426
42451CB00008B/224